SOUL SONGS

A Zora's Eyes Book
Copyright 2001 by Carl C. Chancellor

This book is a work of fiction. Names, characters, places and incidents either are products of the author's imagination or are used fictiously. Any resemblance to actual events or locales or persons, living or dead, is entirely coincidental.

All rights reserved. No part of this book may be reproduced or transmitted in any form or by any means, electronic or mechanical, including photocopying, recording, or by any information storage and retrieval system, without permission in writing from the publisher.

Published by:
Multicultural Publications
P.O. Box 8001
Akron, OH 44320
Printed in Hong Kong
First Printing

Library of Congress Catalog Card No: 00-132-123

ISBN 1-884242-76-6

This book is dedicated to the memories of Calvin and Rosalie Thomas and Harold "Pete" Carmichael.

Special thanks to my family and friends, who through their encouragement and inspiration made this book possible. In particular I want to acknowledge the efforts of Cristal Williams, Tina Garnett, Carla Davis, Carol Cannon and of course the fellas from the old neighborhood
— the Thomas boys, Hall, Robinson, Wells, Curtis, Tony, Bubby, Ronnie, Jackson, Harrison and Mike
— who were always with me in spirit.

LINER NOTES

As a kid growing up in the 1960s, I can't tell you just how many late night hours I spent sitting up in my bed, huddled under the covers, holding a transistor radio to my ear.

Up under those blankets, my thumb frantically working the dial at the side of a palm-sized radio, I would hurriedly spin through the AM band. A cacophony of indecipherable noise, snatches of music and talk, poured from the tiny speakers as I flicked down on the dial, until it had just about run out of room to move any further. At the end of that radio dial is where I found my soul.

If I had lived in Detroit, Philadelphia, DC, or just about any other city, my nocturnal search would have ended up in just about the same place, because at the end of the AM band was where the soul music stations were invariable located.

However, since I grew up in Cleveland, Ohio my thumb only relaxed when it settled on 1490-WJMO or 1540-WABQ.

"*I know you want to leave me, but I r-e-f-u-s-e to let you go...*"; I had to be careful to keep the volume turned down low. The last thing I wanted was to alert my parents that I was still up on a school night grooving to the Temptations, Billy Stewart, the Dells, Aretha, James Brown, the Intruders, Jimmy Ruffin, Little Stevie Wonder, Mel and Tim, the Fantastic Four, the Supremes, Edwin Starr, Smokey and his Miracles, Archie Bell and the Drells...

In the dark, under my covers, radio pressed to my ear, head bopping, body bouncing, I came of age.

I am a true child of the '60s—a time when this country was making its first tentative steps toward a brand new day, marching away from the stark racial divisions of the past and moving along a path where even reaching the moon was within the realm of possibility.

It was a turbulent time that began with fire bombings, boycotts, protest marches and police attacks, as Negroes demanded to be included in America and to partake of its great promise.

It was a time that ended with fire bombings, boycotts, protest marches and attacks on police, as Blacks condemned America for reneging on that promise.

We kicked off the '60s with the prayerful chant on our lips of *We Shall Overcome* which we sang full of hope, swaying from side to side, our arms crossed in front of our bodies and our hands clasped.

We closed the decade with the defiant shout in our mouths of *Say It Loud I'm Black and I'm Proud* which we sang, full of bravado, standing firm to our ground, our arms thrust straight up over our heads, our fists clinched.

Soul music, my music, the sounds of Motown, Philly, and Muscle Shoals, was the soundtrack of that time providing the rhythm, the beat and the lyrics for a decade like no other.

My music, soul music, captured the tenor of the '60s, a hopeful time where events conspired to open up housing, schools, voting booths and, most importantly minds. A time when I believed *Everything Is Alright and Outtasight*.

My music, soul music, reflected the gradual shift in attitude that by the end of the 60s, with Vietnam raging, Attica erupting, and urban ghettoes exploding, gave way to the anti-establishment mindset of *Inner City Blues* and I found myself asking, *What's Going On?*

So all you Soul brothas and soul sistas, git ready to git down to the real nitty gritty, 'cus whatcha bout to git next to, is shonuff mellow and so real, it will make a blind man talk 'bout seeing again.

Now go find yourself a bottle of Ripple, lightcha up a square and cop a squat and I betcha your last money honey that when you finish Soul Songs you be quotin' Marvin Gaye, talkin' bout "Doot-doot-doot-doot-wow! Say, yeah, yeah, yeah. Say, yeah, yeah, yeah."

CHAPTER 1

"KEEP ON WALKING AND DON'T LOOK BACK. Baby, baby baby. Just keep on pushin' and don't look back, hmm, and don't look back. . . ."

"Huh? What?" The pensive look clouding Chance's dark face didn't alter in the least as he stared helplessly at the computer screen.

"Oh, nothing Chance. I was just humming to myself," said X, running his long fingers through his salt and pepper dreadlocks as he looked across the desk at his friend who was clearly befuddled by the almost blank computer screen.

Chance nodded mechanically in response, but it was obvious that he had only grabbed snippets, if anything, of what X had said. He hadn't looked up from the laptop computer, which sat less than a foot away from his nose for the better part of ten minutes. During that time his fingers had barely moved, glued, immobile to the tiny keyboard.

"Dammit, why was this coming so hard?" Chance cursed silently to himself again. He glanced up at the large analog clock that hung on a massive pillar in the middle of the newsroom. The clock clicked and a large green 28 flashed into existence next to the green four that preceded it.

"Shit." This time the curse was audible. For the last 40 minutes Chance had been grappling with what had been budgeted as the lead A-1 story in the next day's Beacon Herald. His editors back in Cleveland were waiting for 45 inches of well crafted color and thought provoking commentary, and he had, what?— all of four, five, six words; that and his byline—Chance Marshall, Beacon Herald columnist.

Chance just shook his head and gave a disgusted half laugh. It didn't make any sense that a veteran newspaper man, with more than 15 years of experience, doing everything from writing obituaries and chasing fires to covering two presidential campaigns and finally writing a column three times a week, pontificating on local, national and world events, was having such a bear of a time penning his personal observations of an event like the Million Man March.

It was an assignment he had lobbied long and hard to secure, despite the objections of the paper's politics writer, who claimed, and rightfully so, that the March was part of her beat.

However, Chance succeeded in convincing his editors that the March was more than a politically motivated rally, it was a spiritual awakening, potentially as powerful in its social significance as the March on Washington in 1963.

"You are talking about a million black men marching on Washington, not asking the government to recognize their grievances, or to acknowledge some Constitutional slight, but to simply proclaim their manhood. These brothers are laying claim to their manhood, individually and collectively, and vowing to accept the responsibility of that mantle. You can't possibly convey the power and majesty of such an event unless you have grown up black and male in America." That argument during a heated news meeting had persuaded his managing editor not only to assign Chance to the story, but also to carve out a third of the front page for his comments. And here he was staring at a blank computer screen.

"The newsroom of the Washington bureau was just too neat," Chance muttered to himself as he attempted to rationalize his present predicament. He was used to clutter, he needed clutter to relax, all this order made him uncomfortable. Things here were too damn organized, too, too... Chance couldn't find the right adjective. He had been unable to come up with the right words for the last half-hour.

Chance's desk in Cleveland was strewn with letters, old papers, stacks of reporter's notebooks, empty soda cans and at least three coffee cups, two of which could have doubled for Petri dishes owing to the film of molasses-like sludge coating the bottoms. But he could put his hands on anything he needed in a matter of seconds.

A Messy Desk Is A Sign of An Organized Mind. That's what the certificate read that several colleagues had framed and hung on the wall next to Chance's desk.

Chance glanced around the newsroom of the Washington Bureau again and grudgingly had to admit that it wasn't all that ordered. Stacks of papers narrowed several aisle ways, sweaters and jackets hung on the backs of chairs and there were several desk tops that would have given Chance's desk back at the Beacon Herald a run for its money. However the desk to which Chance had been directed to set up shop failed to live down to his standards. Clearly, F. Murphy, if the brass nameplate in the right corner of the desk, next to the Garfield coffee cup filled with pens and Magic marker highlighters, all with caps securely in place, was to be believed, was obsessed with organization. There was a dictionary, Roget's Thesaurus, two volumes of famous quotations and an Associated Press style book pressed between two brass soccer ball bookends. The mini-library nudged up against an open Day Planner with several neatly printed calendar entries filling the open pages. The only other addition to the pristine scene was a framed picture of what had to be F. Murphy's family—two red-headed boys, who looked to be about nine or ten, flanking a perky blonde woman, who Chance guessed to be in her early thirties holding an infant in her arms.

Chance caught himself musing about F. Murphy and his family and had to pull himself back from going off on some tangent. He chided himself for not focusing on the task at hand and told himself to concentrate.

Chance eyed the computer screen and started again. He tapped against the miniature keyboard hoping something would jump out and grab him from the string of words flowing across the screen, something profound, something insightful, something nearing poetry that would capture the wonder of that afternoon. He wanted poetry. He wanted to paint vivid colors with his words — words that would bring home what he knew was a special moment in time. He wanted to make his readers feel what he had felt: The spiritual exhilaration of being in the midst of hundreds of thousands of black men and not an angry word being exchanged not a profanity uttered, even in jest. The real sense of caring love and respect that was shared among all these black men evidenced by prolonged hugs exchanged without a hint of self consciousness. What he experienced, what he saw had to be trumpeted, had to be acknowledged, had to be honored.

Instead what had appeared on his computer screen was a dull, straight news account-more than a million men. Black men-professionals, blue collar, retirees, gangbangers, young, old, gay-black men stood in the shadows of the Capitol and the Washington Monument. . .

Sighing deeply, Chance yanked his hands off the keyboard, pushed away from the desk and for the fifth time trudged over to the water fountain.

"Brother, you letting them crackers get to you." X made the observation in a hushed voice, as his friend passed him wiping the water from the corners of his mouth and once again assumed the position in front of the laptop.

As if on cue it started up again. "Epstein, did we get an updated count from the Park Service yet?"

It was the third time in the last 20 minutes that the red-nosed bureau chief, Alex McCarty, had hoisted his bulk out from behind his desk, waddled into the middle of the newsroom and bellowed out the same question to the dozen reporters hunkered over computers, tapping away on deadline stories. This time the big man stared over the top of bifocals perched on his pitted, bulbous nose and fixed his steel gray eyes on weasel-looking Epstein.

"I'm telling you, it's not going over 300 thou. I would stick with 250,000. I think we're safe with that figure," Epstein wheezed loudly between stained teeth. As soon as the gangly reporter finished speaking, both he and McCarty glanced quickly over at the two black men in the far corner of the newsroom.

X wasn't a bit phased, and even Chance did a much better job of masking his annoyance than he had the first two times the fat man bellowed that same question in the middle of the newsroom above the din of television newscasts, the clatter of computer keyboards and the dozen separate telephone conversations.

It was a bit disconcerting to Chance, who viewed his even temper as one of his character strengths, that he could so thoroughly detest a man he had only met a few hours earlier, although he knew the man well by reputation.

Chance had heard stories from reporters, back in his own newsroom in Cleveland from those who had worked with McCarty during part of the man's 18-year stint at the Beacon Herald in the 70s and early 80s. According to the accounts, McCarty had been a hard-nosed, hard-charging reporter who, once he sunk his teeth into a story, wouldn't let go until he had sucked the last bit of news marrow from its bones.

McCarty went after a story as ravenously as he obviously went after a meal, thus his many awards for investigative reporting, including being a finalist for a Pulitzer Prize, and his 300-plus pounds.

However fortunes had changed for the now aging newsman some years ago as the Beacon Herald, like newsrooms across the nation, began undergoing fundamental changes as more blacks and women joined the news staffs.

It wasn't that McCarty was a blatant racist or sexist, at least that was the disclaimer provided by those who related the stories. It was just that the man wasn't adaptable. Once he set his coordinates, he couldn't, or wouldn't change course. McCarty had even refused to yield to the computerization of the newsroom, still in 1995 preferring to type his occasional story, but mostly memos and monthly reports, on an old IBM electric typewriter.

It was a verbal attack on a young female reporter, McCarty called it just a simple exchange of ideas between two colleagues, that eventually landed him in the Washington bureau. Chance couldn't remember the exact dates, he just knew sometime in the early 80s McCarty had fallen out of grace.

When he attempted to defend himself to management, McCarty correctly argued that over the years he had routinely called several male reporters "stupid sons of bitches" and even worse during the heat of deadline pressure when he thought someone had missed an obvious statement of fact, or failed to have a crucial question answered in a story. He just couldn't understand why calling a "gal" journalist, "a stupid, pampered little rich bitch" had been any different. He was astounded that the statement had reached the level of a capital offense.

At any rate, McCarty found himself heading a one-man bureau in the far flung suburban zones of the Beacon Herald. He lingered there for several years until someone decided to kick him up to a low-level assistant assigning editor slot in the Washington bureau five years ago, with the idea that he would just ride a desk until he reached retirement age, which was now just two years away.

But true to form, McCarty had other plans and reverting back to his old news instincts, became a valued asset spooning up all manner of tidbits from the political stew simmering inside the Beltway.

So there he was, a holdover from another era, but still sharp and just has heavy-handed as ever, overseeing the operations of the newspaper chain's Washington bureau.

"Alrighty then, we'll stick with that number in the lead, two hundred and fifty thousand." McCarty let his words float in the air for a moment before grabbing the worn, brown belt wedged under a massive bulging belly. He hiked up his badly wrinkled Docker pants and readjusted his tie, pulling it tight around ruddy, rolls of fat, which oozed over a frayed collar, testifying to the man's excesses, and waddled back to his desk.

"I wonder how many more walks from his desk to the center of the newsroom he got left in him before his heart clamps up on his lard ass?" asked Chance, again readjusting the height of his swivel chair.

"Check yourself out," X said. "You letting these folks distract you from the matter at hand. You got a story to write and you allowing all this penny ante shit to get inside your head."

X watched as Chance flipped through his notes scribbled in a narrow reporter's notebook for the seventh or eighth time, circling and re-circling passages.

"Look here," continued X. "I'm going down to the cafeteria and get me a pop. You want something?" X rose to his feet and waited for a reply, but Chance was finally tapping away again at the keyboard. As X walked by he bent down to Chance's left ear.

"I'll tell you this. When big boy drops in his tracks he better hope that there's somebody else round besides me. Cause I know I'm going to forget them digits. It's going to be like 9-1. . . now what was that last number?"

Both men chuckled at the thought. X moved down the hall and Chance resumed his typing.

"Naw. This ain't getting it." Chance fingered the backspace key and held it down. The dozen lines of type he had just completed were dispatched in reverse order, letter by letter, until the screen was blank yet again.

It was more than McCarty that messed with Chance's ability to concentrate. That was giving the fat man too much credit. No, Chance had questions swirling in his head that he wanted to ask X. Up until running into X that morning during the march, it had been more than 20 years since he had seen his old friend, a guy he had spent almost every waking hour with from the age of seven until they graduated from high school in 1970.

The last time they saw each other was at the funeral of X's mother, five years after they graduated, but they hadn't really spoken then. He told X how sorry he was for his loss and that was about it. The last time they had really talked was during the summer of 1970, right before he left for college and X left for the West Coast.

But his catching up on old times, reconnecting the bonds that had long been broken by years and distance, had to wait until he finished his story, which wasn't coming.

Chance sighed deeply, closed his eyes and lowered his head, the bridge of his nose resting on the back of his knitted fingers. When he looked up he was surprised to see X standing almost in front of him.

"Thought you went to get something to drink?"

"Did," said X, holding out a can of Pepsi for Chance, but before the reporter could grasp it, McCarty bellowed again from across the room.

"Channel 4 is reporting about some kind of disturbance involving some vendors," the fat man blustered while holding a remote in a ham hock paw and aiming it at a bank of televisions.

"What we got on that?" McCarty grunted over his rounded shoulders to no one in particular.

"It wasn't much of anything," offered a young, red-headed reporter.

"The TV's saying it's something, Ms. Leeland," snapped McCarty condescendingly not bothering to look in the direction of the woman, who had now blushed a shade of red even brighter than her hair.

"Dammit, get me something on that altercation. Dammit, get me at least a well-written five inches, something on that disturbance, or any disturbance that can be worked in high in Epstein's main story on the march. I want to lead off with something dramatic, a fight, a confrontation with police, if nothing else some racist blabbering from old Louie Ferry-Can."

The young female reporter startled by McCarty almost asked "what?" but she caught herself in time, and simply responded with a feeble "Okay."

It was X who caught Chance.

Pressing down on his shoulder, and shaking his head "no," X eased Chance, who hadn't realized that he had sprung to his feet, back into his chair.

"Man, do you have to write your story up in here? That's a portable ain't it?" X nodded down to the laptop computer. "So let's hat up out of here and you can write back at your hotel."

While he was making that suggestion, X pressed shut the flip-up screen of the laptop.

"Cool?"

"Yeah. Yeah. It's cool," said Chance gathering up his notebooks.

"I meant you?" X whispered in a calm, steady voice that was meant to lower tension.

Chance chuckled at X's attempt to defuse the situation.

"Since when did you become Mr. Mellow? I can remember the time you would have been ready to throw down. As I recall, I was usually the one cooling you out."

"Hey, my brotha, times change. And so do folks."

Chance thought about that. He wondered just how much things had changed since the days he, X, Biggie, Roach, and O. D. had run the streets of Cleveland. Had it actually been almost thirty years ago? Just how different was he? Just how much had he changed? And what about this country. How was the America of the 60s really that much different than the America of the 90s?

Chance looked over at X. Besides the graying dreadlocks and the glasses, he hadn't changed much outwardly. Nodding to himself, Chance decided that the years had been kind to him, too. Sure it bugged him that his hair, which had gone white at the temples, was thinning but Chance felt his beard, which was also flicked with gray, had nicely balanced out his face. In fact he felt he looked rather distinguished, every bit the sage, intelligent observer of life he fancied himself.

Like X, Chance had kept himself in good shape, the results of three-days a week workouts in the gym and never more than two glasses of single-malt scotch a week. As a matter of fact, since high school Chance had only added 50 pounds to his 5-foot 10-inch frame. A necessary 50 pounds, particularly given the fact that from the age of 18 to about 25, he had barely tipped the scales past the 120 mark.

Thinking about weight brought Chance's thoughts back to the fat man in the newsroom, which also brought back his anger.

"The elevator is here. Chance, the elevator."

It took several seconds for Chance to become aware of the tugging at his elbow.

"Man, you just going to stand here looking stupid?" said X, under his breath as he eased his friend into the elevator.

Chance stared at the fat man and Epstein who were smirking and nodding to one another in private conversation as they eyed his exit. Then the metal doors finally wheezed shut.

A blast of hot, stale air brought Chance back to himself as he stepped from the National Press building. Traffic snaked slowly up a clogged 14th street and a steady stream of people, each intent on their own missions, flowed around the two friends.

"Good thing it ain't night. Two brothers like us would have a hard time getting a cab," joked X, as a taxi eased to the curb.

X ducked in first and slid across the worn vinyl rear seat. Chance followed.

"This is some kind of day," announced the driver in highly accented English.

"Where you from, brother?" asked X.

"Nigeria." The driver spoke over his shoulder as he twisted hard on the steering wheel with two hands and gunned the cab back into the crush of traffic.

Chance, only half aware of the conversation between X and the cabby and even less interested, rolled down the rear window. A blast of hot air ruffled the pages of the reporter's notebook on his lap. He held a pen to a blank page but the story still wasn't coming.

Closing his eyes, Chance tilted his head back on the seat. He tried to write a few lines in his head but his ears wouldn't let him concentrate. They took in the commotion of traffic before they finally fixed on the sound of the flapping notebook pages.

Instead of calling up images of the Million Man March, Chance's mind, cued by the sound of the rustling paper and the hot air blowing against his face, flashed images that he hadn't thought about in years. Yet, there they were in Technicolor, fluttering across the wide screen of his closed eyelids.

"People get ready there's a train a coming. Don't need no ticket, you just get on board..." The Impressions 1962-1964

CHAPTER 2

THE STREAMS OF AIR JETTING IN THROUGH THE wide-open windows of the big, blue 1961 Mercury station wagon did little to cool the car's six occupants.

A film of perspiration clung to the brows of the young man and woman perched on the car's front seat.

The rushing air twisted the thick chestnut hair of the caramel-colored woman, who sat with her head tilted back and propped against the top of the plastic covered seat. With eyes closed, the young woman hummed softly to herself as she absently fanned a paper plate above the placid face of the little girl curled and sleeping in her lap.

The young man, his white, short-sleeve shirt pasted to a widening circle of sweat between his thick shoulder blades, scowled at the road as he worked the steering wheel in one hand and twisted frantically at the radio knob with the other.

"Damn hillbilly music. Is that all they play down here?" He cursed into the car's green-tinted windshield.

"Eugene, the children," chided the young woman, passing the paper plate several times in front of her face and then lowering it to cool her snoring daughter.

Not their father's cursing, nor the twang of country music pouring from the radio reached the ears of the three boys fidgeting in the back seat. The sounds had been drowned out by the whoosh of hot air rushing through the windows as the Mercury zipped along the flat expanse of Florida highway.

The thick plastic covering on the car's seats clung tightly to the sweaty backs of the boys' bare legs.

The colored-ink pages of the Marvel comic books that the boys had been reading had long since been tossed in the back of the station wagon and now fluttered like hummingbird wings in the hot gale.

The highway shimmered in rippling waves. The road's black asphalt, basted in gasoline fumes, pulsated in the summer heat.

Ten-year-old Chance sucked halfheartedly on a Coke. Instead of refreshing him, the warm brown liquid made the oppressive heat even more unbearable.

Adding to his misery was the sweaty, slobbering, head propped on his shoulder.

"Get up off me," Chance snapped at his brother, shrugging a narrow shoulder to dislodge the head.

Bobby woke with a start, grunting to catch his breath. But before he could focus his watery eyes, the heavy lids slid back down. His head wobbled on his neck and he fell back against the car seat.

Slowly Bobby's head, mouth drooling, melted down the plastic seat cover like browning butter working its way down the sides to the center of a hot cast iron skillet, and returned to his older brother's shoulder.

"Ma, tell him to get off me. He's always on top of me. Make him move over. Ma," whined Chance.

Breathing out a deep sigh, the young woman in the front seat, sat up straight, laid the paper-plate fan at her side, and sighed heavily a second time. In a calm, steady voice she addressed her sons.

"Why don't you guys try to sit still and be quiet? It's hot and everybody's tired. You all are tired. Your father's tired and I'm tired. So please just try to get along with each other. OK? I promise we will be out of this car in just a little while." She ended her plea with yet another deep sigh and returned to fanning the little girl.

"But, Ma . . ."

Whipping around, her thick mane of chestnut hair flying across her face, loose strands sticking to the dew on her forehead, Chance's mother leaned over the front seat and cupped his chin firmly in a slender hand.

"Look, I've about had it with your foolishness. Now, you sit back there and keep still. I don't want to hear another word out of you until we get out of this car. Do you understand me?"

So startled by his mother's swift movements and by the unfamiliar sternness in her voice, Chance temporarily lost the ability to speak.

"Do you understand me, young man?" His mother spoke again through clenched teeth, the rounded edges of her red nails dug into the boy's fleshy, dark brown cheeks.

She waited for an answer.

"Yes," Chance whispered.

"What's that?"

"Yes, ma'am, I understand," Chance said feebly, as his mother eased the pressure of her fingers.

Lonnie, head held down to hide a grin, snickered under his breath.

Bobby, still sound asleep, shifted his bushy head on Chance's shoulder, searching for a more comfortable position.

Chance wanted to punch Lonnie dead in his mouth to shut him up. In his mind Chance pictured letting go with a roundhouse blow that would cause his annoying 6-year-old brother to clutch two trembling hands to a pair of bloody, puffy lips. But Chance knew better than to indulge such an urge.

As tempting as the prospect of doing bodily harm to his little brother was it would have been suicidal. The certainty of his father's wrath was something Chance, or any other mere mortal dare risk, particularly since his dad was already pissed at the radio.

Instead Chance chose to examine of the tops of his tennis shoes. He stared down at the scuffed rubber toes, the frayed, dingy-white shoe strings and at the silver eyelets and steamed in silence.

For the better part of two hours Chance had been trapped in the hot box of a car, wedged tight between an unyielding door and his slobbering 8-year-old brother, he would give anything to finally reach their destination.

It hadn't helped matters that his father had already pulled over to the side of the road twice to let his little sister, now asleep on their mother's lap, pee.

To squat down between the cover of two open car doors and relieve herself was a true adventure for Lilly. Of course, when you're four years old, just about anything you are allowed to do on your own is a big thrill.

For the third time during their two-hour ride, Lilly had decided to thrill herself and she wasn't about to cut her pleasure short by letting her brothers rush her.

Eagerly she squatted, with her yellow elbows balanced on two rusty knees and her lacy pink underpants stretched between two match-stick legs. As she peed, Lilly scanned her surroundings, marveling at the huge cottony clouds as they drifted by.

Passing cars and trucks that sped by sent blasts of hot air from beneath the Mercury, warming the girl's bony rump. Lilly's eyes sucked in the flat, green landscape, while the stream she spilled was sucked in by the sandy earth.

Chance hated Lilly's pit stops. But since they were being forced to stop, at least they could have pulled into a gas station, he thought to himself. It didn't make any sense to drive by gas stations when Lilly had to go. At least if they had stopped at one of the Esso or Texaco stations they passed, he could have gotten out to buy a Kit Kat or a Moon Pie, and a cold pop, instead of just baking in a hot car waiting for Lilly to finish.

Hoping to sleep, Chance closed his eyes, and tried to imagine a cold pop a grape Nehi or maybe an R. C. Cola sliding down his parched throat, coating every organ it passed with a layer of frost.

"Damn, I hope we don't stop no more," whispered Chance to himself, upset that he was unable to conjure the sensation of a refreshing, cool drink.

The constant stopping so Lilly could empty her bladder, slowed down what was already a snail-pace trip.

When he and his brothers had piled into the back seat earlier that morning, Chance had been filled to bursting with excitement. He must have read the newspaper ad, which had been reduced to a folded, damp square of paper in his back pant's pocket, a hundred times COME LIVE THE ADVENTURE. EXPLORE THE WONDERS OF THE DEEP IN GLASS BOTTOM BOATS. RIDE THE CLOUDS IN FLORIDA'S LARGEST ROLLER COASTER. COME FACE TO FACE WITH THE WILD CREATURES OF THE JUNGLE AND THE RULER OF THE PRIMEVAL FOREST TARZAN, KING OF THE JUNGLE. IT'S ALL AT SILVER SPRINGS.

Stuffed in a back seat oven, one brother drooling on his shoulder, the other taunting him, the excitement Chance had once felt had long since melted and had settled into a bubbling, gaseous pool in the pit of his stomach. Lions, tigers, alligators, even Tarzan no longer mattered. All he wanted was out of the car.

Lonnie, also tired and anxious to get the trip over, took his mind off the heat and boredom by tormenting Chance. Sometimes he would swing his feet and "accidentally on purpose" kick his oldest brother. Sometimes he'd make faces, sticking out his tongue. Or, he would dig in his nose and threaten to fling a booger. This time Lonnie employed the wayward feet and booger combination.

"Stop it, punk," hissed Chance.

The whispered threat only encouraged Lonnie, and he stepped up his teasing.

"I said stop it, punk!" Chance had spoken much louder than he had intended.

Immediately, Chance sucked hard at his bottom lip, held his breath and looked in terror at his father.

Even from the back he could see the muscles at his dad's temples pulsating under the pale skin, which, much to Chance's dread, was quickly turning red.

His father's stubby fingers, like ten, tiny boa constrictors, squeezed the steering wheel. The tension of his grip reverberated through his beefy hands, up both hairy arms and across his broad shoulders.

"Damnit, Jan, keep those kids quiet," he growled, gnashing his teeth.

The angry timber of his father's voice rudely shook Bobby out of his slumber.

"Wah, what's going on?" stammered Bobby, his eyes blinking rapidly and still half asleep.

"Are we there?" Bobby slurped at the spit in the chalky corners of his mouth, rubbed his eyes and scanned the flat landscape beyond the car's windows.

"Mommy, I don't see it. How much farther do we have to go before we get there?" he sniffed.

Chance couldn't believe what he was hearing. Was Bobby out of his mind, blubbering on like he was? Hadn't Bobby seen their father's pulsing red temples? Shut up, fool. Just shut up, before you get us all in trouble, Chance pleaded silently to himself. Please, just shut up.

It wasn't until Bobby, still trapped in the fog of sleep, glanced at the look of horror in his brothers' wide eyes, that he finally snapped to consciousness. The danger had at last registered, but had awareness come too late?

All three boys held their breath and waited for the explosion.

Chance's lungs were ready to pop and still nothing had happened. He glanced puzzled, first at Lonnie and then at Bobby. His look was met with the same questioning stare in the eyes of his little brothers.

The explosion hadn't come. It hadn't come!

The boys were floored. Jan was grateful that the prayers of a mother, tossed so hurriedly to heaven, had been answered. She jumped swiftly on the unexpected reprieve.

"Now, you boys quiet down and play a game. It will help the ride go faster and before you know it we will be there."

Lonnie and Bobby heeded their mother's advice and played license plates.

"Indiana! New York," blurted Bobby.

"Georgia," said Lonnie, returning serve, as the big, blue Mercury sped past a brown Rambler.

Chance sulked and stared out the window. He had no desire to play license plates, or Password, or Hang Man, or the Match Game. His bladder was full and aching. His stomach was queasy. He was hot. He was tired. And he was way past ready to get out of the damn car.

It was then, as he wallowed in his misery, that he saw it. At first it was just a slender outline, barely discernable against the bunched clouds. Slowly, the outline took on definition as the Mercury drew closer.

It was a man with long, wild, black hair that rested on broad, bare shoulders. The man clutched a long knife in a raised fist. His other hand pried at the jaws of an agitated alligator.

Then the blur at the bottom of the billboard, just under the gator's scaly, green tail, materialized into letters and then into words SILVER SPRINGS 20 MILES STRAIGHT AHEAD. OCALA EXIT.

Lonnie and Bobby noticed the sign too and put their game of naming license plates on hold.

The Mercury blew quickly by the 20-foot tall wooden ape man. The boys snapped their heads around to look again at the billboard as it shrank in the tailgate window.

They had hoped to glean more details about the wonders of Silver Springs and of the King of the Jungle. Instead, they read a ditty about Burma Shave that was on a sign topped by the silhouette of Tarzan's head and raised dagger.

"How long will it take to drive 20 miles?" asked Bobby, pressing his mother for details.

She calmly shifted the girl in her lap from the crook of her left arm, to her right and gently brushed aside threads of brunette hair that fell in the sleeping girl's face.

"We should be there in about 30 minutes or so. Not much longer."

"What time is it now?" asked Lonnie, placing his moon-shaped, yellow face on top of the front seat near his mother's shoulders.

The boys' father huffed and angrily twisted at the radio's tuning knob.

"It's 11:15 now," said their mother, glancing at the thin silver watch circling her wrist. "Now, sit back and be patient," she cooed, hoping that the subtle meaning of her words was understood.

Somehow the news that there was indeed an end to the trip, and it was only 30 minutes away, lifted Chance's spirits. Almost immediately his stomach stopped hurting and the heat was not nearly as oppressive. Chance sunk back into the stiff plastic and daydreamed about the wonders of Silver Springs and most importantly, Tarzan King of the Jungle.

"What time is it, Mommy?" asked Bobby.

"It's five minutes later than the last time you asked," she said and again offered her warning. "Now, just sit back and be quiet. We will be there soon."

Still swimming in his imaginings of ferocious lions, thrashing gators, and of Tarzan swinging from vines yelling his yell—Ahhhhhh Yeee Ah Yeee Ahhhhhh, Chance didn't pay much attention to the exchange between his mother and Bobby.

"Are we almost there?"

Chance heard the words, but at first wasn't sure where they had come from. Then he felt his mouth moving again, and to his horror realized that he was the one who had made the foolish inquiry, and what was worse, he was about to ask the same question again.

A warning flashed in his brain: Shut-up! Shut-up! Chance tried to choke back the words, but it was as if he were possessed. For some reason that he couldn't understand, he no longer had control over his mouth. If he had, he would have pursed his lips closed and clamped two hands over them to make sure they remained that way.

To Chance's great dismay, he heard himself again.

"How long before we get to Silver Springs?"

Out of two wide eyes, Chance watched as his mother just shook her head in a way that made her thoughts obvious: "Lord, why did you give me a fool for a son?"

"Damnit. Didn't your mother tell you to sit back and shut-up?" The voice of the man behind the wheel filled the car, rattling the handles of the doors and windows along with the metal flaps of the ashtrays.

Bobby and Lonnie scooted as far away as they could from their insane older brother.

The demon that had taken over Chance's body had fled too, leaving the curly headed boy to face his father alone.

A pair of eyes, narrowed under the weight of furrowed skin that bunched to form a series of vees above the bridge of a red, flaring nose, burned out at Chance through the rearview mirror.

"Boy I'm just about three seconds off your butt" His father's temples pulsated red as the eyes bore deeper.

Eyes watering from effort, Lonnie tried to restrain himself with all the willpower his 6-year-old body could muster, but his yellow cheeks puffed with air that uncorked a spray of spit and laughter.

"Oh, so you want some too, Lonnie? Don't make me pull this car over and come back there. I promise that you won't think it's so damn funny then."

His father's growls, although they weren't directed at him, nonetheless twisted on the faucet in Bobby's eyes. Tears zigzagged down his face and snot bubbled from his nose.

Sulking, Lonnie sucked in his stomach to trap his giggles and shot a murderous look over the hands he pressed hard to his mouth, at his eldest brother.

Turning away from the indicting stare, Chance laid his face on the top of the window slot in his door. The hot, humid ribbons of air beat hard at the boy's face. Finally, he succumbed to the relentless pounding and drifted off.

The popping sound of gravel crunching under the big blue Mercury's tires shook Chance awake. Bobby and Lonnie were excitedly pointing skinny fingers at the hand-painted posters of wild animals and exotic birds that lined the park's entrance.

As the Mercury rolled slowly up and down the lines of parked cars, their mother pounded with a brush at the rude mass of hair that danced wildly atop Lilly's bobbing head.

"Sit still girl and let me get this mess straight on your head."

Lilly let out a little yelp, as her mother popped her thighs with the wooden back of the brush. From that point on, the little tender-headed girl sat still and endured her beauty treatment.

"Now, I don't want any running when we get out of the car and I want everybody to stay together," announced their father as he eased the

Mercury into a narrow gap created by a dark green Cadillac and a faded out pick-up truck.

"Ready?" He turned off the Mercury's engine and glanced over at his wife, who was still fighting with Lilly's rambunctious hair.

"No, I'm not quite together yet. I know the boys can't wait so why don't you go ahead and we'll meet you at the front gate."

Before she finished speaking Chance and Lonnie had their doors open.

"Mommy, I can't find my shoe. I can't find my shoe." The sound of panic filled Bobby's voice and tears again filled his eyes.

"Now, don't go and work yourself up. Just take your time and look. Your shoe has got to be back there somewhere. Did you look under the seat?"

"Chance, you and Lonnie help your brother find his shoe," their father ordered.

The two boys moaned in disgust. Chance cursed under his breath. Lonnie, accidentally on purpose stomped on Bobby's hand as the sniffling, boy crawled over the potato chip and Frito-littered carpet to hunt for his lost Red Ball Jet sneaker.

"Eugene, why don't you go ahead and take Lonnie and Chance? I know they're ready to get out. Bobby can come with me and Lilly when he gets his shoes on," said their mother gripping Lilly's frowning face in both hands as she inspected her grooming effort.

As soon as their father's hand touched the curved, silver door handle, Lonnie and Chance exploded out of the car and raced across the lot, kicking up gravel and dust.

"Young men, what part of don't run' didn't you understand!"

Instantly, the two boys skidded to a halt. Before the dust particles had a chance to start their descent back to Earth, their father had grasped both boys tightly by the hands and marched them down the row of cars. Whenever he sensed the urge rising in either of his boys to hurry the pace, he applied a firm squeeze to suppress the notion.

"Did you boys roll up your windows when you got out?"

Lonnie nodded yes. Chance dropped his chin to his bird chest.

"Go back and roll up that window right now. I don't know where your mind is, but I do know you better get yourself together in a hurry. You are the oldest and you should be the one setting an example for your brothers. I just don't know about you sometimes. You worry me."

Chance wanted to protest. He didn't want to turn around now that he was so close to Tarzan, King of the Jungle. But Chance knew it was useless to argue with his father, so he pivoted and trudged back to the car.

After only a few steps Chance glanced over his shoulder, hoping to see his father and Lonnie waiting patiently for him to return. They hadn't. Lonnie and his father were nearly at the turnstiles.

"What are you doing back?" asked his mother when Chance arrived at the car. She was kneeling in front of Bobby's feet, which dangled from the back door, as she laced up his sneakers.

"Daddy told me to come back and roll up my window."

"I already did," announced Bobby.

Before Bobby finished, Chance had already bolted, running full-out back up the lot.

As he bounced along, he scanned the horizon for his father and little brother. He finally spotted them standing near the turnstiles talking to a man in a white pith helmet.

"Sure is a real hot one today," said the pith helmet, mopping his pock-gouged ruddy face with a crumpled blue rag.

"How much will it be for two adults and four children?" inquired Chance's father.

"Well, let's see now. That's two at eight dollars, and four at. . ."

"Daddy! Daddy!" shouted Chance, interrupting the figuring of the pith helmet, as he neared at full gallop.

The pockmarked face flushed crimson and his rheumy eyes widened.

"Now, now there ain't no colored allowed in here," the pith helmet blustered, his slack cheeks puffing in and out.

"Where is y'all from?" he asked, still blubbering.

The same shade of blood red rose in the face of Chance's father. His temples pulsated so that it seemed his skull would split from the pressure.

Lonnie desperately tried to pull his hand from the tightening vice of his father's grip.

The pith helmet retreated three steps back from the heat of hate and anger that radiated from the narrowing eyes that threatened him.

"It's policy. I don't make the rules. I just follows them. Y'all, y'all gots your own park, a very nice park, just for coloreds less than a half mile down the road." The words bumped into one another as they rushed forward from the pith helmet's thin, cracked lips.

Chance peered at his father, but wasn't sure he knew the face he saw.

His father's narrowed eyes poured a deep boiling hate into the pith helmet. His blood pulsed red just under the surface skin of stretching taut across his face.

For a long moment the world fell away, all but the four-foot square of dirt shared by Chance, Lonnie, his father and the wizened white man.

Then his father turned his back on the pith helmet.

"Let's go." The words were barely audible trapped as they were behind clenched teeth.

Lonnie, being dragged behind his father, was mute and confounded. He was not alone.

What had happened, Chance pondered as he tried to make some sense of what he had just witnessed. Why were they leaving? Why hadn't his father exploded? He wanted, he needed answers.

His racing thoughts were interrupted by the sound of snickering at his shoulder. Chance turned to see a sawed-off freckled face white boy under a mop of orange hair.

The white boy's mother gathered him closer and shook her blonde head as she turned to whisper to the lanky, owl-faced man beside her.

It seemed to Chance that the whole park was whispering and pointing white fingers. He wanted to plant his right sneaker all the way up to the blue star emblem at the shoe's ankle, into the white boy's spotted mug, smashing his pug nose until it spread across his alabaster face in a pasty red mess.

Instead, he followed wordlessly in the angry wake of his father.

Chance's mom, Bobby at the end of one hand, and Lilly tethered to the other was puzzled by the rapid approach of her husband and sons.

"Let's get back in the car," she said to Bobby and Lilly.

"But, mommy. . ."

"Shush baby. Just do what mommy says."

"But why we getting back in? I don't want to go back. I want to go to the park." When Bobby began to wail uncontrollably, Lilly joined in.

"Shush now. It's going to be alright. It's going to be fine." She hummed softly as she unlocked and opened the door she had just shut.

Wave Skipper II was painted in scrawling faded, white letters along the side of the flat boat moored at the end of a rickety, weathered pier. A very large, very black man stood on the boat's deck.

Two of the three boys in the back of the big, blue Mercury, which minutes ago pulled to a stop on a dusty patch of sunbaked dirt passing as a parking lot, stared longingly at Wave Skipper II. Chance refused to be pulled from his thoughts and didn't even look at the boat.

"Do you want me to tell you what they can do with their damn Silver Springs? I have half-a-mind to drive back to Tallahassee right now."

For the last five minutes, the young woman, who resumed fanning Lilly with a paper plate, had tried to reason with her husband.

"Eugene, the kids really want to go. They have been riding all day. A boat ride will be relaxing for everybody."

Her husband huffed.

"Look, if you and the kids want to go then go ahead. I don't feel like going, okay?" Her husband growled drawing out each word as he struggled to control his tone and his temper.

His wife drew in a deep breath that lifted her shoulders before it exited her body in a low, whispered sigh. She turned to her sons and instructed them to walk down to the boat and wait.

"You three keep up with your sister. Hold Lilly's hand," she said fixing her eyes on Chance. "Your father and I. . ." she fixed the same no nonsense look on her husband, "will be down in a minute. You just wait for us there."

As the four children approached a very large, very black man bellowed.

"Ahoy, mates. Y'all ready to sail with Cap'n Sam?"

"Our mommy said to wait here. She and my dad will be along directly," piped Lonnie.

"Well, I guess if them is your orders, you best to follow them to the letter," said Captain Sam in a heavy, rich voice that rose from the pit of the great belly that oozed over his thick belt.

"You chilrens ever been on a glass-bottom boat before?" The captain, wistful tufts of gray hair creeping from under a battered white baseball cap stained with a yellow band of sweat, waited patiently for an answer.

"Tain't too talkative, is y'all? That ain't no never mind. I does enough talkin' for a whole passel of folks," said Captain Sam, jumping from the boat onto the splintered, gray pier. He kneeled next to Lilly and rested two, ham hock hands gently on the little girl's shoulders.

"You sure is a powerful pretty little thing. I bet your name is Susan. Naw, Mary. Naw, naw, that ain't it." The captain wrinkled his brow and rubbed at the white stubble that dotted his chins with a fat thumb and finger.

"I know, your name is Bertha Mae."

The little girl peeled in laughter.

"It's Lee-Lee." A wide toothy grin, which sported a few empty spaces, spread across her tan face.

"Well, it's a pleasure sho enuf and a honor to make your acquaintance Miss Lee-Lee," said Captain Sam, doffing his cap and revealing a swath of shiny pate.

"Here comes your mother and dad now," said the Captain as he stood and replaced his cap with a flip of the wrist.

He greeted the young couple warmly. The woman returned the Captain's welcome with an even warmer smile.

Her husband didn't acknowledge the Captain, but stood stone-faced, his hairy arms folded across his chest.

"Y'all ready for a real adventure? I tell you it is somethin' special when you sail with old Cap'n Sam. Somethin' special."

The Captain, extremely nimble for such a massive man, bounded onto his boat, which bobbed in the water under his considerable bulk.

"Well I know I'm ready. How about you guys?" The young woman tired very hard to infuse excitement into her words. With a brush of her hand she herded her children toward the boat.

Captain Sam extended a beefy paw, offering boarding assistance.

"Sit wherever you want. Cause, as y'all can see, you be my only passengers." Captain Sam laughed a laugh the rolled up from his toes and out through his gaped-tooth grin. He spread out his arms and bowed, bending at what on anyone else would have been a waist, but not on this block of a man, and offered up his vessel.

The Wave Skipper II hadn't been much to look at from the pier and had even less to distinguish herself once on board. Running along both sides of the boat were a set of rough-hewn wooden benches, stained a tobacco juice-brown that had been buffed to a high gloss by countless colored back sides.

At the base of the benches, stretching nearly eight feet along the length of the boat, were two large panes of thick plate-glass, boarded by an 8-foot by 4-foot slender brass railing supported at each corner by three-foot high wooden posts bolted fast to the deck. The glass bottom offered an expansive view of green tinted water.

The only portion of the boat not covered by a faded blue and white striped, canvas awning was a wooden folding chair, with high legs, which was also bolted fast to the deck in the boat's bow.

Captain Sam took his position, standing at a wooden wheel next to a platform of buttons in the stern of the boat.

He reached down and threw off the thick, twisted mooring rope and punched at the buttons. The engine gurgled and coughed plumes of white smoke. Foam spilled from underneath the boat and long plumes of seaweed swayed in the panes of glass.

The engine coughed again, let go of three quick burps of black smoke and then roared to full power. Foam boiled up and rode atop the churning water at the back of the boat.

A ribbon of a million, tiny silvery bubbles, like crystal beads, raced across the glass. Palms of sea grass bent back and quivered as Wave Skipper II chugged slowly from the pier.

"Child, why your face all screwed up?" asked Captain Sam looking over at Chance as he guided the boat out into the wide, calm river.

The boy shrugged his shoulders. The Captain shot a knowing glance at Chance's mother.

"Look at dem white folks over there, all crowded up and cramped on that boat. Well, they'll be lucky if they see two or three fishes," said the Captain, nodding at a boat that could have been the twin of Wave Skipper II.

The white man at the wheel of the glass-bottom filled with white folks trolling the other side of the river, waived at Captain Sam.

The Captain grinned a 100-watt smile that was a phony as a three-dollar bill and waved back.

"He don't know nothin'. They hires all these young crackers, most of them college boys home from school for the summer. Let me tell you they don't know nothin' 'bout this here river. Nothing. I expect that they would have a hard time gettin' wet if they fell in.

"Lawd, y'all lucky to be wid me, cause I done gone and forgot more 'bout this place than all them crackers over there on the white side of the river ever thought about knowing."

Captain Sam waved at another boat load of white folks. In all, there were three boats, overflowing with loud crackers plying the waters.

"They ain't seein' a thang 'cept maybe a few blue gills and a catfish or two, who be too lazy to swim to my side of the river. All that commotion them crackers keep up scares most of the fishes away. And the gators. Lawd, these gators don't want nothin' to do with their foolishness," Captain Sam informed his six passengers.

The Captain twisted the wheel sharply. The flat boat wheezed and spat out white foam as it dipped deep to one side, putting distance between it and the noisy whites.

"Careful there baby, we don't want you going overboard," Captain Sam warned Lonnie, who was laying on his belly on the flat bench, leaning both arms over the side trying to scoop up foam.

"Boy, you better sit up. Or do you want to sit over here next to me?" As the young woman spoke she patted a hand on the bench next to her and Lilly.

The Wave Skipper II was silent now, except for the gentle slapping of water against her sides, as it skimmed over the still, glassy surface of the river.

Lifting his cap and dragging an ashy forearm across his brow to rub away beads of sweat, Captain Sam craned his shiny head out over the boat's side and launched a huge glob of spit into the water. He froze at the edge of the boat, lips still pursed, hoping his pose would add drama to the question he was about to ask.

"Can y'all spit?"

Bobby and Lonnie quickly responded to the challenge. Both boys sucked in their cheeks, filling their mouths with as much saliva as they could hold, and simultaneously let fly with spit wads of their own.

Lilly screwed up her face in disgust and buried her eyes into the warm curve of her mother's arm.

"Come on, y'all can do better than that. I bet if you tried you could probably hit one of them boats over there."

The Captain grinned at Bobby and Lonnie spitting themselves dry.

The spitting pushed the day's earlier disappointment from the two boy's minds. Lonnie and Bobby eased to the deck of the boat, their faces almost on the glass, as they searched wide-eyed for the creatures that the Captain pointed out in the green-tinted world under the boat.

Lonnie, Bobby, Lilly, and even their mother, ooowed and aahhed at the wonders of the river. Lilly, was so startled by the sight of a two, thick, puffy gray lips, which rocketed from a forest of sea grass to kiss the bottom of the boat, she broke out crying.

A deep belly laugh rumbled through Captain Sam.

"Don't be frightened honey, that's only old Gus the Grouper. He's just a big ol' flirt who loves him some pretty girls."

Chance, his lips poked out as far as Ol' Gus', had no intention of letting Captain Sam pry him loose from his disappointment and anger.

NO COLORED ALLOWED.

The words smacked Chance over and over again upside his black, black head. As much as the words hurt, he refused to let go of them. He should have just spat them out into the water and let the current carry them away. But instead he chose to suck on them and let their sour taste drip down the back of his throat.

No colored allowed. That is what the buck-toothed cracker had said and he said it looking directly at him, thought Chance. The picture of the man's nasty, red pitted-face, his beady-blue eyes shaded by the brim of the pith helmet was seared in his mind. It was an image that grew even more intense in detail when he closed his eyes to block it out.

Those accusing, pin-prick blue eyes, full of scorn, had looked Chance up and down. Chance knew those eyes were angry at the fact that they had been fooled by the light-skinned man holding the hand of that little yellow boy, both of them with almost straight hair. Those eyes could never reconcile themselves to the fact that they had carried on a conversation with a nigger without ever realizing it. That coon would have certainly gotten into their park if that tar black boy hadn't shouted, "Daddy."

It was all his fault that they hadn't gotten into the park, Chance told himself.

It was his fault that they weren't riding the rides, eating candy and popcorn.

It was because he was so damn dark that they weren't watching the King of the Jungle battle lions, gators, and hordes of savages with bones through their noses and plates stretching their lips.

The moment the pith helmet looked at Chance and stopped him in his tracks with those words, it was like Tarzan himself had plunged a knife deep into him.

Chance had been so shocked that at first he didn't comprehend what was being said or what it really meant. All he knew was that the ground under his feet seemed to be pulling him down and he was keenly aware of the air being sucked out of his lungs.

Still, he hadn't panicked, because he knew that his father would straighten everything out and get him to Tarzan. After all his father was a lawyer, a well-respected man in Cleveland, and it was just a no-account honky barring their way.

When Chance saw the anger boiling in his father's face and the wrath it always foreshadowed, he almost felt sorry for the white man in the pith helmet. Almost.

But when his father only stood and stared, even after the red had filled his face, and then snapped around on his heels and stormed away, it confused Chance, and he wasn't sure what had taken place.

It still made no sense to him. The only thing he was certain of was that because of his black face, he and his family were sitting in a raggedy-ass boat on the damn colored side of Silver Springs.

Chance glanced over at his father, who sat silent and motionless at the rear of the boat. The blood that had surged in his face, turning it an angry crimson, had cooled and thickened underneath the skin that had turned to marble. With brow deeply furrowed and eyes closed, his father tilted his stone face upward to the sun.

No more than four feet of space lay between them, but Chance sensed that his father was worlds away from everyone else in the boat, and even further away from him.

CHAPTER 3

WORDS SEEMED TO ALWAYS BE AT A PREMIUM when it came to interaction between father and son.

Just four months after the incident on the glass bottom boat Chance came home from school to a Corlett Moving van in the driveway. His father sat behind the wheel of the big blue Mercury station wagon which was filled with boxes, odds and ends of furniture—a rocking chair, two plastic covered hassocks, lamps with their shades stacked on the front seat, two old child-sized, cane bottom chairs and several suitcases.

"You and Bobby hurry and put your books up and change your clothes. I want you two to help your mother pack some boxes and put them out on the tree lawn. I will be back in about 15 minutes and I want to have some more stuff ready for me to load up in the car." As soon as their father finished, he eased the car from the curb and headed slowly away, the wheels spinning out a low hum which grew higher in pitch as the car moved faster down the red brick street.

Chance looked at Bobby. Bobby looked back at Chance. Both boys turned and headed across the lawn to the front door of the house. They were almost knocked down by two men balancing their living room couch between them.

"Watch it little fella. You almost got runned over," said the tall, breaded man at the far end of the couch. The man, more precisely the huge butt that had bumped into Chance, knocking him into Bobby nearly sending both boys to the ground, just grunted, not even looking back to see what damage his rear end might have caused. Steadying the couch against his equally large belly, the Butt slid one of his hands from the couch, tugged at his pants pulling them up so only an inch of booty crack showed. He then readjusted his grip, nodded at the bearded man three couch cushions away and headed to the moving van. They carefully steered their load between the hedges and the brick-lined flower bed that bordered the narrow walkway from the drive to the front steps.

"Chance, you and Bobby get out of the way and come in here and help me get packed," said the boys' mother, a film of perspiration on her brow and dampening the bottom edge of the scarf tied tight on her head.

Chance and Bobby eased through the doorway and put their lunch boxes on the kitchen table that was now sitting in the living room.

"Don't you see that they are coming to get that table so why would you put you lunch boxes on it?" She didn't wait for an answer. "You two go change you clothes and start putting your toys in boxes, Lonnie is already in there."

Lonnie was in the room but he wasn't rounding up toys and placing them in the three cardboard boxes that sat at the foot of the bunk bed.

"I know something you don't know," teased Lonnie from the top bunk. Chance and Bobby ignored him and started picking up toys.

"I said, I know somethin' you don't know."

Bobby turned to look up at Lonnie and was just about to ask "What?" when Chance jumped in.

"We already know. So there, chump."

Bobby looked at Chance in amazement. Now, he was even more upset. What did everybody know that he didn't?

"You don't know nothing, Chance," Lonnie challenged.

"I do too know."

"No you don't. You don't know nothing. You don't know…"

"I know you three better stop playing around and do what I told you to do," said their mother who had materialized in the doorway to their bedroom, one hand on her hip, the other holding an old diaper that had found new life as a dust rag.

Seeing the questioning look in her two oldest boys' eyes she stepped into the room.

"Didn't your father tell you when you were out by the curb that we're moving?"

The statement hit Chance harder than the Butt that had shoved him off the steps minutes earlier. It was all he could do to stammer out– "What do you mean moving? Moving where? Why?"

"See, I knew you didn't know," chimed in Lonnie as he scurried down from the top bunk.

Chance shot a quick menacing look at Lonnie, but was too shook by what he had just heard from his mother to do anything more.

When Lonnie reached the floor his mother flung the dust rag over her shoulder and pulled him close to her. She then reached for her other two boys and all four of them plopped down on the lower bunk.

"We are moving to a new house, a much larger house, so you boys won't be jammed into one small room. As a matter fact, Chance you will get your own room, and Lonnie and Bobby will share a large room. And you won't have to sleep in bunk beds if you don't want to."

"Will we be going to the same school?" asked Bobby, not quite sure how he felt about Chance getting his own room and him still having to share with Lonnie.

"It's just around the corner. So we will still be in the same neighborhood. You will still go to the same school, and you will still play with your same friends."

She could see that the boys still wanted to talk, but she refused to get side tracked.

"Look, we don't have time to discuss it now. Your dad will be back soon and he's going to want to start loading up the car again. So do what I told you in here and when you get finish Chance and Bobby come out here and start taking the boxes I've already loaded to the curb."

"What about Lonnie? He's big enough to help, too."

"Lonnie is going to help you two in here and when he's finished he is going to play with Lilly in the backyard so I can get something done."

"That ain't fair."

"Chancey Eugene I don't want to hear it. I've got no time for your foolishness. You just do what I told you to do and keep your mouth shut. Do you understand, me young man?" she said as she rose from the bed, keeping low so not to bump her head.

Lonnie started giggling.

"But Ma."

"Chancey Eugene." His mother burned his name into him with her narrowed eyes. She only used the detested Chancey when her eldest had stepped on her very last nerve.

But her husband had never been a fan of the name, calling it country when his wife had first suggested it as a possible moniker for their first born. She wanted her son to be named after her favorite relative, Uncle Chancey Combs, who she remembered as being the most dapper man in Nicholasville, Kentucky.

Chance's father secretly figured that her favorite relative had gotten his name because someone on his wife's family tree couldn't spell Chauncey.

However, despite getting his way on almost everything else, Eugene Marshall's wife had refused to budge and he grudgingly acquiesced to her wishes.

While, Chance's mother had won the battle, her husband won the war. From the first day he held his son, Eugene Marshall shortened Chancey to Chance. It wasn't until Chance was seven years old did he learn his real name, and just like his father, promptly discarded it.

Chance didn't say another word and started picking up toys.

His mother hadn't lied about the new house. It was almost twice as big as the little cape-cod brick house they had left on E. 154. Although Chance wasn't crazy about the loud yellow color, he couldn't get enough of the two huge pine trees that flanked the walkway leading up to the front door.

When he and his brothers had first seen the twin green monsters hunkered up close to the house, as they carried boxes up the front steps, their minds immediately started racing. However, their mother was the one who always won those races and applied the brakes to her sons' thoughts.

"There won't be any climbing of these trees."

"You got that right. I ain't got the money to pay for a bunch of broken bones," added their father as he brushed by hefting two large boxes, the one on top trailing a flowered bed sheet that curled around his shoulders.

"I better not hear of anyone climbing these trees." When their father spoke, he never ended with the question "Do you understand?" like their mother did. He knew his children clearly understood that they better understand or suffer the consequences. That put an end to all thoughts of ascending the Marshall pines.

"Hey, don't I know you? Ain't you in Mrs. Wamsley's sixth grade class?"

Chance looked hard at the talking apple tree. It had just tossed one of its green offspring at him, which burst in a spray of juice at his feet.

"Yeah," he shot defiantly back at the tree, which had shook loose a skinny, charcoal black, nappy headed boy from its branches. The boy produced a green apple, which also splintered in a rain of juice when it hit the driveway near Chance.

"Thought so. I'm in the room across the hall, 112, Mrs. Joneses," said the boy bouncing yet another apple between his hands as he moved forward on two stick-like ashy legs that seemed to make up three-quarters of his body.

"I'm Lindsey, Lindsey Harris," said the boy flipping the apple over his shoulder and extending a hand toward Chance.

"Yeah, but we call him Roach," said the apple tree again. This time it produced two more bodies.

"Go to hell," said Roach as the two other tree boys approached.

"This here be O. D. and Biggie," said Roach making the introductions. Chance nodded his head to acknowledge the two new boys, but said nothing.

"Boy, ain't your mama taught you no manners?" asked O. D. shrugging his heavy shoulders and looking to Roach and Biggie for a possible explanation for the new kid's rudeness.

Still it was a full ten seconds before Chance spoke up and gave the trio his name.

"Saw y'all when you moved in Friday. Was going to wait till we got back to school to see if it was you. But I thought it was you. I knew you looked like the kid in Old Lady Wamsley's class," continued Roach.

"Ain't that major work? You one of them smart kids," cracked O. D., the question coming out as a challenge.

"Where your brothers?" asked Roach, trying avoid any conflict, at least just yet.

"Who? Bobby and Lonnie? They went with my moms to the store," answered Chance still a bit uneasy.

"You got to hang round here or can you leave?" Roach continued.

Chance thought about that question for awhile. No one had exactly told him to stay in the yard, but he had told his mother that he didn't want to go to the store because he wanted to stay and fix his bike.

"Fix it, but don't go riding anywhere. We'll be back in a little while." Those were the words, as best as he could remember, that his mother had spoken to him before driving off. Chance didn't recall her saying anything like "don't leave the yard". She had only said not to go riding his bike anywhere.

"Man, this dude can't be in no major work, he too slow," said a smirking Biggie, who slapped five to O. D.

Chance wasn't sure about his new companions. He recalled seeing all three boys in the hallways of Gracemount Elementary School and thought he had even taken a gym class with the yellow, freckled-face boy called Biggie.

"Naw, I don't got to hang round here. Where you all going?"

"We was bout to head over to O. D.'s pad to play a little b-ball," Roach stated, bending down to tie his sneakers, a pair of well-worn, dingy red P. F. Flyers.

"You live next door?" asked Chance looking down at Roach.

"Naw, that's the Johnson's crib. They've been out of town and we've been watching X's apples," said Roach, standing again and nodding to the apple tree where the three had been perched just minutes ago.

"X?" asked Chance.

"Yeah, he hangs with us too. He should be back in a week. He went down south for a funeral or something," added O. D.

"I wished somebody up and die in my family so I could miss a week of school," whined Biggie.

"Don't be saying that. That be bad luck. Man, don't be messin' with stuff like that." The concern was real in Roach's voice.

"Man, I'm just playin'," Biggie said shrugging off Roach's warning.

"Bigs, don't be playing like that. My Auntie Mosey say you be conjuring up bad spirits talking bout death and such." Roach almost whispered the last part of the statement.

"Man, are we going to play some b-ball or what? I'm ready to get it on," complained O. D.

"Sounds cool to me." Chance walked by the trio to close the garage door. He consciously affected his baddest pimp, a slow-paced walk that required him to almost drag his left leg while leaning to the right and swinging his right arm.

O. D., Roach, and Biggie looked at one another but didn't have any immediate reaction.

"Yo, Chance where's that basketball I saw you bouncing in the drive the other day? Why don't you bring it along? O. D.'s ball all slick and ain't got nuff bounce," said Biggie.

The remark ticked O. D. off just a bit because Biggie was always cracking on somebody and anyways, he thought, wasn't they supposed to be messing with the new kid?

"I wouldn't worry bout that too much because if you playing against me and O. D. you won't be touching the ball much no way," said Chance, who had quickly decided to get the biggest of the kids on his side. Chance could see his remark had worked by the smile turning up in the corners of O. D.'s fleshy lips.

"I heard that, Chance. These two rookies ain't got a prayer," barked O. D. The fat boy, who outweighed Chance and Biggie by at least 50 and Roach by a good 100, extended a beefy, callous paw. Chance slapped the massive kid some skin, which instantly evaporated the tension.

Then the woof-tickets started to fly fast and hard. Roach would crack on O. D. and O. D. would crack on Biggie, and Biggie on Chance, with the light-hearted round robin of insults running the gamut as the four new friends headed to the backyard ball court.

CHAPTER 4

FOR THE PAST FOUR DAYS THE STRESS HAD BEEN GROWING in the large yellow house, pushing out at the walls, pressing up from under the floor boards, rumbling up the two flights of steps into the attic straining the roof trusses threatening to shake the house off its foundation.

Yet Chance remained determined to hold his ground. He was adamant that this summer he wasn't going to Tallahassee and nothing was going to alter his mind.

Every summer since he was eight Chance spent the first three weeks of August with his grandfather and grandmother in Florida.

The first couple of years he couldn't wait to be packed up and shipped off. He would worry his mother to death, working on her last good nerve as he impatiently counted down the days to his departure. Chance couldn't understand how it could be that June and July, the first two months of summer vacation, could possible stretch out like they did, the days barely slogging by.

Going to visit Grandma Esther and Partner, as Chance's grandfather enjoyed being called, had always been a great adventure. At the top of that adventure list were the vivid tales Partner spun of growing up in Texas "reared rough and ready by the cowboys" he would boast in a deep voice that seem to rumble up from his feet.

"I'm talking bout colored cowboys, son, and let me tell you, they were the real deal." Partner made that statement without so much as batting an eye, said it just like it was a well known fact.

The first time Chance had heard his grandfather make that pronouncement, he felt himself rolling his eyes up into his head. But Chance was able to control that reflex, not wanting to be smacked for being disrespectful. Still, he was nonetheless a bit insulted. He wasn't a little boy who needed to be entertained by fairytales. Chance knew good and well there weren't any Negro cowboys. Chance couldn't believe that Partner would feed him such nonsense.

Partner saw the doubt in his grandson's face but refused to acknowledge it and just kept on with his story.

"Was a Negro cowboy who invented bull dogging. You ever hear of the Buffalo Soldiers boy?" Partner continued without so much as a pause. Nor did he wait for a reply before going into the story of the famed 9th and 10th Cavalry, U. S.

Chance was polite and listened but it bothered him that Partner would treat him like a little kid. If there had been Negro cowboys he would have seen somebody like him, someone with dark skin, who wasn't wearing feathers, riding to rescue a wagon train in the movies or going after the bad guys with the Lone Ranger, or The Rifleman on television.

"Boy, what you don't know could fill two box cars."

His grandfather's words caught Chance short.

Wrapping two large hands, the veins as thick as rope fanning out under the age-spotted skin, over the well-worn arms of an overstuffed leather chair, the old man pushed himself to his full height of just under six feet. But as he steadied himself on a massive ebony walking stick, the cane topped by a brass head of a long-horn steer, he seemed much taller. As he stood still for several seconds, allowing for his arthritic knees to adjust to his still solid and compact 198 pounds, he appeared to grow even taller.

Sure of his feet underneath him, Partner strode in a wide, flat-footed gait to the dark cherry bookshelves that lined three walls of the cramped room. The thin scent of Old Spice cologne wafted in the old man's wake.

Several hundred books, a dozen or so framed diplomas, certificates and honorary degrees, several old photographs, a mounted pair of buck antlers from which dangled a large 10-gallon Stetson hat, and the heavy cherry wood desk, buffed to a high gloss which showed through in the tiny areas not covered by papers and more photographs, all combined to make the room seem like it would collapse in on itself from the sheer weight of its contents.

Partner, his bald pate rivaling the sheen of the desk, plucked a book from among the rows of leather bound text in various shades of browns, which stood at differing heights on the shelves. He tossed the thin volume in his grandson's direction.

"Read," was all Partner said as he marched out of the room, the cane that he almost never used for walking, clamped tight under his right arm.

For the next three hours Chance rode herd with the likes of Bill Pickett and brought settlers, who carried all their worldly goods in Conestoga wagons, safely out West with the 9th.

When Chance wasn't being carried away by his grandfather's stories, he would join the Harriston kids, four boys and three girls, nearly carbon copies of one another, to explore along the railroad tracks that ran through the woods behind his grandparent's house.

When Chance and the next-door Harriston clan weren't following the rails, they were crawfishing or out on mock hunts for rabbits and birds, which they would try to bag with homemade bows and arrows, slingshots and boomerangs.

Even the daily chores of collecting eggs, feeding the feisty chickens and helping in the garden, Partner's " big spread" as he called it, was exciting.

Still, what Chance liked most about being in Tallahassee, aside from his grandfather's stories and Grandma Esther's white mountain cake, were the sand covered streets. The tan grit, more than ankle deep when you twisted your foot down into it, snaked through the black section of town. Of course it wouldn't be until his fourth summer visit that Chance even realized that Tallahassee had a separate black section.

"I don't understand. You used to love going to visit your grandma and grandpa. You couldn't wait to go and now you're telling me you don't want to go? This doesn't make any sense whatsoever." The words bumped up against one another as Chance's mother spoke them. With arms crossed tightly in front of her, she leaned in the doorway of her eldest son's room and shook her head in exasperation. Until that moment she hadn't fully understood just how much she looked forward to this break, shipping her three sons to her parents. And next year when Lilly turned seven, she would join her brothers, too.

It gave her three glorious weeks to escape from the 24-hour demands of motherhood. An opportunity to shed her "Mommy" skin and get to know herself again, the person she was before becoming cook, maid, doctor, referee, teacher and miracle worker.

And who knows, maybe this year she'd get her sister Reba to keep the baby and she and Eugene could take a little get away trip and reacquaint themselves. That is, of course, if he could tear himself away from that office long enough without feeling that the place would fall apart without him there.

Who was she fooling, she mused to herself as she slid out of the doorway and glided over to the scarred oak dresser. She hummed to herself in a low whisper as she arranged the mass of odds and ends-cologne bottles, hairbrushes, stocking caps, a large can of Duke hairdressing, its center scooped out, a dozen Jet magazines, and several 45s-strewn across its top into some semblance of order. She knew her husband would never take a vacation from that job and could hear him scolding her. "I am the first Negro lawyer ever hired by the Cleveland Electric Light Company and I'll be damned if I'm the first Negro lawyer they fire."

No, the very best that she could hope for was to keep him from going into the office on the weekend. But even that possibility would be shot down if she didn't get Chance to Florida. She knew if he stayed home then Lonnie and Bobby would want to stay, too. Bobby, because he was never fond of Tallahassee anyway, always whining about the heat. Lonnie, because he would be worried that Chance was getting something he wasn't if he weren't around to protect his interest.

She hadn't expected this rebellion from her oldest son and it was upsetting. However the only outward manifestation of her inner turmoil was her delicate humming as she straightened the dresser top.

Having tried to reason with him, cajole him and bribe him with a raise in allowance, she had finally been forced to resort to the threat—"I'm going to let your father handle this."

She had hesitated using that hammer. She had hoped to avoid employing that ultimate weapon, particularly since she spent a great deal of energy, almost daily, trying to protect her children from the wrath of their father.

When Chance heard his mother use the threat, he finally realized just how serious the situation was and how important his going to Florida must be to his mother.

The specter of his father's anger hung out there like the hydrogen bomb, both equally frightening and dangerous.

It seemed like his entire life had been lived under those dual, ominous shadows.

In school he had watched countless filmstrips about the H-bomb. He had practiced the Civil Defense drills with his class, walking briskly and quietly in double file down the hallway to the basement of the school where they would "press shoulder to shoulder, duck and cover."

Chance had even seriously entertained the idea of asking his father to build a fallout shelter in the basement of their home. He had written a short speech and to back his request had two handouts he had gotten from school "You Can Survive An Atomic Blast" and "Be Safe Not Sorry," both of which outlined how to build and outfit a proper fallout shelter.

However, Chance decided not to risk making his father angry. Although he couldn't figure why anyone would get upset by something that made so much sense, particularly since every family in America was building a fallout shelter.

Still, rather than pushing the button with his father, Chance decided it would be much safer to run the three blocks to Gracemount elementary and hunker down in the school's basement when Russia attacked.

Compared to his father, the bomb was just a threat, something that may or may not come to pass. However, he had been at ground zero on numerous occasions when his father exploded and he had somehow survived the fallout, at least thus far.

So it puzzled Chance that he wasn't more unnerved by his mother's threat of fatherly intervention.

No, Chance had set his mind on spending this summer in Cleveland and that was that.

After all he was a big city Northern boy. No, make that a man. He was 13 and was too cool and way too sophisticated to be spending his summer stuck with a bunch of backwoods, countrified Negroes. He needed to be with dudes like himself. He needed to be hanging out at the outtasight happening places like the Red Carpet lounge down on the "five," East 105th Street, and Leo's Casino up on Euclid Avenue.

As a matter of fact, Chance had already made plans to checkout the Temptations and Booker T and the MG's, who were headlining at Leo's August 3 through the 7th, exactly the time he was supposed to be in tired ass Tallahassee.

"Uhuh. No. It ain't happenin'."

"What?" His mother asked as she turned from the dresser and looked at Chance who sat on the edge of an unmade bed.

Chance hadn't realized he had spoken out loud.

"Ah, nothing Ma. Nothing."

Caught in the high beams of his mother's eyes, Chance had to stop and think about why he wanted to stay in Cleveland this summer. To tell the truth it had come as a surprise to him that he was so staunch in his resolve not to go to Florida. The fact was he had truly enjoyed his summers in Tallahassee, not only because of Partner's stories and the outdoor adventures, but also because of how he felt, felt deep inside when he visited.

He felt superior–superior because he was from the north and from a big city like Cleveland. He enjoyed bragging about going to the Browns football games and telling the Harristons about having actually met Jim Brown, the best player ever to strap on a helmet. Bubba and Cal Harriston, who were one year older and one year younger than Chance respectively, were particularly impressed since they both considered themselves great athletes.

Chance liked how the Harriston girls were in awe of his record collection. The 45s that he carefully packed in their own carrying case, each vinyl disk in its own brown paper sleeve, every time he came to Tallahassee.

"I need my tunes since y'all don't have no Soul stations like we got back in Cleveland," said Chance the first time he lugged his record collection down South with him when he was 11. He remembered his bird chest puffing out in pride when Marvelous Harriston, who Chance had a secret crush on and was always looking to impress, asked; "You got a colored radio station up there?"

"We've got two stations and all they play is Soul music." Chance did a quick James Brown shimmy in the dirt to emphasize the point. He immediately regretted the dance step when Marvelous snickered, signaling that he had perhaps overshot cool and may have landed smack dab on goofy. When Renny and Lil Will, at 5 and 7, the youngest members of the Harriston clan, broke into their own imitations of James Brown, his fears were confirmed and Chance felt his face flush.

That embarrassing moment not withstanding, Chance never tired of taking the records and his portable record player out to the corrugated tin covered lean-to at the back of the Harriston property, where he took center stage. He would plug the phonograph into the extension cord wrapped around one of the wooden poles of the shelter, stick a wad of gum on the back of a penny and attach the penny to the tonearm of the record player, which stopped the record from skipping. With the music blaring Chance would show the Harristons, mainly Marvelous, who in Chance's estimation more than lived up to her name, the latest dance steps. Whenever, Bubba or Cal would question any of Chance's dance moves, knowing that he was showing off for Marvelous' benefit, he would simply counter by saying "That's the way we do it in Cleveland," which was enough to silence his two critics.

Chance liked the way he felt around the Harristons, which went deeper than the sexual electricity he experienced when he looked at Marvelous, whose big, light brown eyes were surpassed only by her breasts. None of the girls that he knew back in Cleveland who were his age could fill out a blouse like Marvelous and certainly none of them had let him squeeze their tits like Marvelous had one day when they had been alone out in the lean-to.

But the good feeling Chance had when he visited Tallahassee had nothing to do with lust, or Marvelous, it had to do with feeling special. It had to do with feeling superior.

Chance felt superior, not only to the Harristons, but to all the folks that lived in the Tallahassee, in the South, because he was a northern boy, a kid from the big city, and he liked that feeling.

That all changed the previous summer.

Up until then the south that the civil rights movement was fighting against, only existed for Chance in the black and white images flashed on the Huntley and Brinkley evening newscast or in the high-gloss pages of Ebony and Jet Magazine.

Partner had always made an effort to shield his grandchildren from the ugly realities of segregation when they came to visit. When Chance, Bobby and Lonnie weren't playing in and around their grandparents' home, hanging with the Harriston kids, they were on the Florida A&M campus, where Partner taught modern agricultural science. Just like the neighborhood where Partner lived, the FAMU campus was an oasis from the ugliness of the South. It was a world where there were no whites only signs, a place where highly educated Negro men and women were in charge. A place where they didn't have to dim their individual lights in difference to anyone.

It had taken a while, but reality finally burrowed its way into Chance's soul. The first punch was delivered as he sat in the back seat of Grandma Esther's Chevy Impala, as he waited in the parking lot of the Piggly Wiggly grocery store where she had gone to shop.

Across the road from the grocery store eight black men, linked ankle to ankle hacked at the thigh-high weeds edging the blacktop with sickles and rakes. Their eyes were downcast, their motions were slow and labored. The sun was a woolen shawl nailed onto their shoulders and sweat poured off their bent bodies. Their white uniforms, a thick black stripe running down center of their pant legs, were soaked and clung to them like soggy wallpaper. The gang worked in silence as two white sheriff's deputies, who sat in a pickup truck, sucked on bottles of Coke as they watched impassively from behind mirrored aviator glasses.

Hot juices bubbled in the pit of Chance's stomach and he felt as if he were chewing on cotton. He wanted to turn away, he didn't want to look anymore but he couldn't. His eyes were pasted to the men, his body chained to theirs. It wasn't until the car door slammed after his grandmother snuggled in behind the wheel, pushing a grocery bag into the passenger seat, that Chance was paroled.

A week after escaping the chain gang, the day before he was to leave to go home back to Cleveland, he had gone into town with two of the Harriston boys and their father, Big Will. Mr. Harriston pulled Chance to the side and warned him to be mindful to enter any building through the colored entrance.

"If you don't see a sign that say colored, you just wait until Bubba or Cal come. As a matter of fact you stick close to Bubba and Cal and don't go doin' nothin until you checked with them furst."

Chance nodded that he understood.

For most of the afternoon things went well. Chance stayed close to Cal and Bubba as they snaked through the aisles at Woolworth's and later stood out front of the Post Office while Mr. Harriston went in. But there was a burning in Chance's pocket and the $10 his daddy had given him when he left Cleveland was begging to be spent.

The last stop of the day was Belks. A department store that Cal and Bubba bragged on as having "some bad rags." Chance doubted it, owing to the fact the little store couldn't begin to compare to Higbees or the May Company back in Cleveland. Still, he figured he could find something, maybe a Banalon shirt, or a silver plated ID bracelet.

Cal interrupted Chance's mental shopping spree.

"Now don't touch anything unless you gonna to buy it. And don't go tryin' nothin' on neither," warned Cal, who flashed yet another warning with his eyes. The last thing Cal needed was some smart ass northern boy asking him why? Cal knew that Chance knew exactly why. Cal also knew if Chance asked the question, he would be doing so just to rub his nose in it. Trying to make him feel small because of the rules he and all other Negroes had to live under down South.

Chance had no intention of embarrassing them both and at any rate, Cal could have saved his warning, since five minutes after entering Belks a prune-faced, blue-haired woman, *Miss Kirby, Saleslady*, said the name tag on her lemon yellow blouse, gave both boys the same lecture almost verbatim that Cal had given, only much louder and more shrill.

Miss Kirby, her pinched face, dotted with brown liver-spots that peeked out from under the rouge caking her sunken cheeks, standing in front of him instantly brought back painfully memories. For Chance it was like he was back sitting in the stern of Wave Skipper II. The same feelings that had rocked him then, a mixture of confusion, anger and helplessness filled him. It was a bitter gruel that made the muscles of his lower jaw ache in spasms.

Weeks after his encounter with Miss Kirby, when he was long since back in Cleveland, the pain and anger lingered. It wasn't like the first time, that time in Silver Springs. Then he was hurt that he couldn't see Tarzan and angry that what he had wanted had been denied.

This time he was angry at himself for being a Negro.

What he had felt during the encounter at Belks department store was like some type of contagious infection. It took up refuge deep inside him and made him ache. Try as he might he just couldn't shake that nagging feeling of being different, of being an outcast.

For months after, whenever he rode the rapid train downtown the sickness made Chance aware that he didn't want to cross the Cuyahoga River to the west side of the city. The white side of the Cleveland. It didn't matter that he wasn't crossing the river, he had planned to end his travels at the Terminal Tower downtown. Chance knew he had never before consciously warned himself against crossing the Cuyahoga.

Even when he went downtown shopping in Halle's and Higbees, Chance had the uneasy sense that the clerks were watching him. Maybe they had always watched him. He had no way of knowing. But he did know that the Miss Prune-Face Saleslady lecture was now being conveyed telepathically to him by every store clerk he saw.

No, he wasn't going back to be reinfected. This summer he wasn't going to be made to feel like—a nigger. The word tore deep into Chance and images of angry white faces, yelling the word at kids in Little Rock, at the Freedom Riders as they ran from firebombed buses in Mississippi, at Martin Luther King Jr., as he marched through Chicago. Chicago?

This summer he was putting his foot down and was going to tell his mother that he wasn't being shipped off to no plantation. He was going to tell her he was 13, a man and didn't have to do anything he didn't want to do. At least, that is what Chance said to himself. To his mother his exhortations came out as whines—"I just don't want to go, Mom."

"Why are you doing this to me? I just don't understand," said his mom again, totally exasperated as she walked out of his room closing the door behind her.

That night at the dinner table Chance's mother eased up to the subject of Tallahassee.

Bobby and Lonnie snickered under their breath. Bobby nearly launched a mouthful of mashed potatoes as he tried to stifle a laugh as he thought about what was sure to befall his older brother.

Chance's mother had second thoughts about mentioning her son's resistance, she really didn't want to see him caught in the vortex of her husband's anger. Still, she needed the break, so she sighed deeply and pressed forward.

"Chance said he didn't want to go Tallahassee this summer."

The statement sat there just like it had pulled up a chair and hunkered down for dinner, its elbows on the table. The clang of Lonnie's fork clattering to the kitchen floor started time back into motion.

Chance closed his eyes and gritted his teeth. Refusing to be fooled by the delayed reaction, Chance remained tensed, mentally hunched into a ball, tucked and covered.

"Bobby, pass me the corn."

Bobby's head jerked up off of his chest. His eyes, flung wide open, bounced from his mother and then to his brothers, looking for a cue as to what to do.

Reaching out to receive the bowl of the Jolly Green Giants nibblets from Bobby's shaky grip, Chance's father scooped out two loaded spoons of corn and dumped it in the empty space between the mashed potatoes and the half-eaten fried chicken breast. "Well, it seems to me," Chance's father continued, pausing to skewer several kernels on the tings of his fork.

"Seems to me if the boy doesn't want to go, then he shouldn't have to." With that he clamped down on the corn and pulled the fork back clean.

Still, it was several minutes before anyone else sitting at the table moved to resume eating.

"Baby everything is alright, uptight, clean outtasight..."
Little Stevie Wonder – 1965-1967

CHAPTER 5

CHANCE CROONED, JUST A BIT FLAT, WITH EDDIE, DAVID, Otis, Paul and Melvin the Temptin' Temptations. He smiled watching his reflection in the mirror that hung from the closet door arms chopping, knees pumping and head bobbing.

"*If you want to play hide and seek with love, let me remind you. It's alright.*
But the loving you're going to miss in the time it takes to find you, is out of sight. . . ."

The reflection spun. Chance dropped to one knee. The reflection jumped up and did a 360-degree spin.

"*Tweedly di, tweedly dum, look out little baby cus here I come. And I'm bringing you a love that's true, so get ready, get ready, cause here I come. Get ready cause here I come. . .*"

"Stop all that bouncing up there," Mr. Marshall yelled, his voice banged off the side walls of the stairwell, turned sharply at the top of the steps, rushed down the narrow hall, and barged into Chance's bedroom.

Chance was too keyed up to pull himself off the stage. His reflection marched in place, keeping in step with the invisible Temptations.

When the saxophone wailed, Chance dipped slightly and slid, to the left, his left foot twisting on its toes, dragging along a stiff right leg. His reflection disappeared into the mirror's chipped, wooden frame.

"Boy, don't make me come up there." His father's deep voice burst into Chance's small bedroom again. This time Chance responded.

Mumbling under his breath, Chance mimicked his father's voice "turn it down," as he twisted the volume knob of the powder blue Westinghouse radio, which sat on his dresser under a pair of underpants and a white sock.

Camel walking to the closet, Chance pulled down a pair of gold, sharkskin trousers from a hanger. The shiny material bounced back the light of the bare 60-watt bulb stuck in the ceiling of the closet as he slung the pants over a thin, brown shoulder.

"All right. All right. That was the mighty Temptations, with a big-en that everyone's dig-en and this is yours truly, the often imitated but never duplicated. Your daddeyo on the raddeyo, Tony O'Jay and I'm coming right back atcha with another one just like the other one. Guaranteed to put a wiggle in your hip and make your back bone slip. The Four Tops with Sugar Pie Honey Bunch. . ."

Humming along with the Tops, Chance rifled through the clothes, which were arranged in rows on hangers. He pushed the unwanted garments quickly aside, sending them sliding down the metal closet rod. Chance stopped several times to consider shirts to compliment the trousers draping his shoulder.

He rejected a burnt orange cotton shirt and then a chocolate brown one, both with heavily starched high-boy collars that stood three inches tall.

He paused at two more shirts before reaching the end of the row of hangers.

Perplexed, Chance reversed the process, this time the search was much more intense, but proved just as futile.

"Damn," cursed Chance as he dropped to his rusty knees to rummage through the pile of clothes laid in little mounds on the floor of the closet. Tossing socks, shorts, and sundry other garments, he still couldn't find the shirt he was looking for.

Still on his knees, Chance crawled the four feet to his bed and peered underneath. He stuck in an arm to probe the darkness and extracted a sweatshirt, a white Converse Chuck Taylor high top sneaker, and several mateless socks.

"Damn!" he cursed again pushing up off the cool wooden floor before padding heavily down the hall, as he held tight to the towel wrapped around his waist.

"Where's my yellow high-boy shirt?" Chance demanded, striding into his brothers' bedroom.

Lonnie and Bobby, stretched out on a frayed brown rug playing Monopoly, ignored the entrance of their older brother.

"Four, five, six. You landed on States Avenue, with three houses. Let's see, you owe me four hundred and fifty dollars." A toothy Cheshire cat grin spread across Lonnie's oval face as he made his announcement.

"Let me see that card," said Bobby, snatching the dog-eared deed from Lonnie's hand.

"My shirt better not be in here," warned Chance, flinging open the door to his brothers' closet. An avalanche of clothes, books, shoes, toys, two footballs and a Danny O'Day ventriloquist dummy, cascaded forward and spread around Chance's bare feet.

"If my shirt is in this mess, I'm going to hurt somebody," roared Chance, sorting through the mess with his foot.

"Get out of our room!" yelled Lonnie, his property deeds stuffed in his shirt pocket. Tucking several hundred dollars worth of rainbow colored bills into the waistband of his pants, he got up from the floor to go to the closet.

"I want my yellow high-boy shirt. I'm telling you, you punks better not have my shirt."

"We ain't got your funky shirt," said Lonnie, kicking the pile on the floor back into the closet.

Bobby seized the opportunity created by Lonnie's distraction from the game to grab two five-hundred dollar bills from the plastic tray of play money. He slipped the two stolen bills into the middle of the multi-colored stack in his hand.

"Man, get out of our room. We can't come into yours so stay out of ours," said Lonnie, shoving Chance.

"Yeah, why don't you get out. You messing up the game," Bobby chimed in.

"Push me again, punk," Chance snarled at Lonnie.

"Mom ! Mom! Chance up here messing up our room! Mom!" Bobby yelled loud enough so his parents could hear him downstairs.

With that Chance grabbed Lonnie in a headlock and the two boys tumbled onto the bottom bunk bed.

Bobby jumped to his feet to join the scuffle and landed two solid punches between his big brother's shoulder blades. The blows switched Chance's attention from Lonnie to Bobby.

As he lunged at Bobby, Chance felt a sudden rush of cold air between his legs, then a stinging pop on his hips.

Lonnie was just about to snap the damp towel again on Chance's butt, when their father appeared in the doorway. The three boys froze.

"Damnit, what's all this foolishness going on up here?"

"Daddy, Chance came in here and. . ."

"Boy, did I tell you to speak? Sit your sorry butts down on that bed right now," their father roared, the look in his narrowing eyes pressing the three boys closer together on the bottom bunk.

"But, Dad, Chance was the one. . ."

"Dummy, didn't I tell you once to be quiet? Now, don't make me have to repeat myself again. Do you understand me?"

"Yes, sir," the three boys said feebly in unison.

The angry heat of their father's shadow fell over the boys as he stepped closer.

"Where are your clothes, boy?"

Fright had made Chance forget his nudity, but having been reminded, he reached for his towel, which he started to snatch from Bobby's hand. Fortunately, he caught himself in time and slowly slipped the towel from his brother's grasp instead, and wrapped it back around his waist.

"Bobby, I want you to tell me what's going on."

"Well, Chance, he, he, he, he came, he came. . ." Bobby struggled hard not to stutter, which was next to impossible when he was excited, angry, or at this particular instance, scared.

Bobby, took a deep breath and tried again.

"Chance came in here te, te, tearing up stuff and throwing it all around the room."

Lonnie co-signed by nodding his head and pointing at the pile in front of the closet.

"Pick up this mess now and put it where it's supposed to go."

"But, Dad, they. . ."

"I don't remember asking you to speak, young man. I told you to clean up that mess," said the boys' father, popping Chance at the side of his head to assist him up from the bed.

"I don't care who made the mess. I told you to clean it up." Chance sulking walked to the pile his father following on his heels.

With their father's back turned to them, Bobby and Lonnie stuck their tongues out at their brother when Chance cast a vengeful look over his shoulder at the two.

Their father snapped back around on his heels.

"You two. Put that damn game away and get ready to take your showers so you can go to bed."

The two young boys wanted to protest. It was only 7 p. m. and it was a Saturday, too. Whoever heard of a 10-year-old and a 12-year-old going to bed so early? Even on a school day they didn't have to be in bed until 9.

Lonnie and Bobby, their eyes watering, knew that their father's edict wasn't fair. If this had been a court of law, the boys knew that their premature banishment to bed would have been overturned on appeal, after all, it was Chance who started the confusion.

But, this wasn't a courtroom. And in Eugene Marshall's house, the only law was his law.

"I thought you told me you had somewhere to go this evening?" The man fixed his eyes on his eldest son.

Chance gave an affirmative nod as he pulled a sweater over a wire hanger.

"Well, I suggest you get yourself together in a hurry and get this mess cleaned up before I change my mind." With that the boys' father padded down the hall and descended the stairs.

Kicking the last of the clothes from the pile into the closet, Chance turned toward his brothers as they slowly took off their clothes.

"I'm going to get you punks. I'm going kick both your asses," growled Chance in a tight whisper.

"DAD!" yelled Lonnie.

Chance hurried from the room, readjusting the stocking cap on his head as he jogged down the hall, stepped into his room and closed the door.

Plopping down on the bed, Chance pulled on his underpants. He sat silent and motionless for five minutes, it took that long for Shorty Long to put him back into a party mood.

"... *there's 007 the private eye and he's bringing all the cats from I Spy. So come one, come all, we're going to have a ball, down at the function at the junction... You betta come on right now...*"

Chance turned up Shorty Long on the radio, and Shing-a-linged into a pair of lime green slacks, a white high-boy shirt and a lemon yellow Alpaca sweater. He was bending over, pulling on a pair of green thick and thin silk socks when there was a knock at his bedroom door.

"Yeah, who is it?"

"It's me, my man." X stepped into the room.

Chance didn't know why X bothered to knock. Ever since they had moved next door to the Johnsons, X had made the Marshalls' home his home.

Glenn and Lydia Johnson would have gone unnoticed on the block, which they would have preferred, being as they were extremely private people who barely spoke to one another, let alone their neighbors, had it not been for their only child Xavier Dominic Johnson.

X had made himself known to everyone on the street by making everyone's home his own. Folks could never really tell you exactly when X first started showing up at their breakfast or dinner tables, just that one day when they asked for someone to pass the girts, or the greens, X's pale hands would be handing them the bowl.

No one ever objected to X's presence in their homes because, well because, he was X. He just seemed to blend in somehow, maybe because he never seemed to take up space. Whatever little extra space there was to occupy, X made sure he fit.

Just two months after moving into their new house, at Lonnie's birthday party, X made himself fit into the Marshall household. It wasn't exactly at the birthday party, which wasn't exactly a party, since only Lonnie, Chance, Bobby, Lilly and their parents had gathered in the kitchen for cake and ice cream.

Everyone was a bit surprised when there was a knock at the back door and the neighbor boy was standing at the door with a small wrapped package in his hand. They weren't surprised so much by X's presence, but by the fact that he clearly had come prepared for the celebration with a present.

Lonnie's surprise turned to disappointed when he unwrapped X gift only to find four colored pencils, which had obviously been used. Lonnie had to be pinched by his mother to offer a mumbled "thank you."

It was X and not Lonnie who soon put the pencils to use. After downing three pieces of cake and two bowls of ice cream, X headed upstairs with Chance and his brothers to draw comic books. It was well after 10 that night, when Mr. Marshall finally said "Good night, Mr. Johnson."

The next morning X was back at the Marshall's kitchen table drawing pictures of the Dare Devil, Spiderman, and Captain America, which he sketched with Lonnie's colored pencils between bowls of Frosted Flakes.

Unlike X, whenever Chance had gone missing from the house for hours or missed showing up at the dinner table, his mother would dispatch his brothers to track him down. If he missed his " when the street lights come on" curfew, the phones at his friend's homes would start ringing until she had located him and advised him "you better get your butt home before I hang up this phone boy."

No, the Johnsons never concerned themselves about the whereabouts of their son and some wondered if they ever noticed X at all.

Chance had overheard some adults whispering about the Johnsons on several occasions, commenting on Mrs. Johnson's poor health and of her husband's job schedule that seemed to have him at work all the time.

Old man Johnson worked the third shift at the Post Office, which was another reason X stayed out of the house, so his stepdad could sleep during the day. His mom had always made it point to make sure that X wasn't underfoot so that Mr. Johnson, as his mother called him, could get his rest. Although his mother had never said so, X took being underfoot as being in the house, so he made it a point not to be in the house.

Mr. Johnson took X's absences as the boy simply avoiding him, which in the beginning bothered him. Mr. Johnson was already well into his forties when he married X's mom, who was just 22, with a 4-year-old boy in tow. He thought of the day he was introduced to Lydia by the sisters at Mt. Zion Missionary Baptist, as the luckiest day of his life. He was ready to get married and have a family, but because he was so painfully awkward around women he thought the opportunity had passed him.

But there she was, a good-looking red bone woman with chestnut hair that hung down in heavy ringlets brushing her shoulders and best of all, a woman in need of a good provider and a father for her boy. It was the last description that the Mt. Zion sisters pressed before they formally introduced Mr. Johnson to X's mother.

They sold Lydia on Mr. Johnson by noting he was a hardworking man with his own house and no female skeletons in his closet.

"Child, he ain't no womanizer and that's about the best you can say about any man," observed Sister Lennie Jordan, who went on in great detail and with flourish to talk about her "no account, skirt chasing husband."

Lydia didn't need much selling. She knew she had a small boy to raise and she knew she needed help to do that. If the man the sisters were going to introduce her to had a steady, decent paying job, that was all she really required. Any other positive traits would simply be icing a cake she didn't have.

Mr. Johnson on the other hand took no convincing at all, not after he saw Lydia, her fair skin and long good hair. She was a dark-skinned, nappy haired, country boy's dream come true.

Any reservations or questions that he had, particularly about the boy and who his daddy was, disappeared when Mr. Johnson saw Lydia.

Three months after their introduction Lydia Mosely and Rayford Johnson were married.

At first Mr. Johnson took his new wife's silence as shyness.

"The hardest work I do all day is pulling a few words out of you gal," he used to joke. As the years passed the jokes had turned into complaints and finally into a stony silence.

Still in the beginning, Mr. Johnson had hopes of having a happy family, which included little Xavier, a boy whose constantly flapping lips more than made up for his mother's silence. The boy had always been filled with a thousand and one questions that he rattled off one after another. Mrs. Johnson worried that her son's questions would annoy her new husband and she discouraged X from bending his stepfather's ear.

"Boy go somewhere and let Mr. Johnson have some peace."

Mr. Johnson, would have objected to the boy being sent away, but he was hopeful that his wife's few words, although not directed at him, would eventually stretch into a real conversation.

When he finally realized, some three years later that trying to get his wife to talk to him was a no win proposition, he decided to concentrate on building a relationship with X. But by then X, used to being shooed from the house when Mr. Johnson was around, had already gone about establishing a life outside of his home.

"It's a shame how that boy has to raise himself," observed Mildred Robinson, who lived across the street, one morning when she was having coffee with Chance's mother. The two women looked at each other for a long moment, idly spooning their coffee, and then burst out in laughter.

"Mildred, I think everybody on the street is raising X," said Chance's mother, unsuccessfully trying to suppress another giggle.

"I wished I knew Mrs. Johnson's secret. I would sure like to pawn my brood off on someone else," she continued, blowing into her coffee.

"Yep, X is an official member of the Marshall family," Chance thought to himself as his friend pushed through the bedroom door.

"Man, I see your pops is in one of his good moods. I thought he was going to go upside my head when I came in," said X, slapping five to Chance and then stepping to the mirror to preen.

"Whatcha do to piss him off?" X continued.

"Hey, you know it don't take much."

"Dig that. But what specifically did you do this time?"

"Them punk brothers of mine mess with my stuff and I get in trouble."

"So what else is new? You got any smell-good?" X asked, changing the subject as he adjusted the collar of his shirt.

"Yeah, up on the dresser next to the radio."

"Man, how do you find anything in this room?" asked X looking under T-shirts and underwear. Uncovering the cologne, he twisted the gold plastic cap from the bald head of a green, glass Buddha and poured some of its fragrant liquid contents into his palm.

"This Jade East is some good shit," said X, patting the cologne to the sides of his face and under both arms.

"It ain't going to take the place of no bath," snapped Chance.

"I got your bath, boy."

"And I got your boy, punk."

Gingerly inserting his fingers under the edges of his nylon stocking cap, Chance pulled the edges out and carefully lifted it from his head. Smiling at the results reflected in the mirror, he tapped a few unruly strands of hair back down into the rows of gently rising and ebbing, Royal Crown-greased, black waves.

"Yes, yes, yes. Mama's joy, mama's joy," proclaimed Chance as he generously splashed on a few handfuls of Jade East.

"Man, bring your tired, no-dressing, punk ass on," snickered X, nudging Chance aside so he could command the center of the mirror.

"We supposed to be hooking up with the fellas in about 10 ticks," said X, adding-"Damn, I'm one pretty muthafucka."

Chance shouldered up to his friend, who was resplendent in a red knit shirt, that sported white cloth buttons and white piping, red sharkskin pants, red silk socks and black Stacy Adams loafers.

Both boys admired their reflections.

"Damn, we some sharp Negroes," Chance observed.

"You ain't never lied, my man. You ain't never lied."

CHAPTER 6

THE HANDS ON THE GOLD FACED LONGINES WATCH stabbed at Biggie, pushing him past annoyance and that much closer to anger.

"Damn that Roach! It's almost 5:15. How much longer we gonna wait for that fool?" Biggie growled the question as he sprung from the steps of the old schoolhouse and stalked off toward the street.

"I don't know why Biggie keep walking down to the corner. It ain't gonna get Roach here no faster," observed O. D. tapping a Kool package against the back of his hand and pulling out a cigarette. He shifted his eyes over to X as he extended the pack and shook up the brown filter tip of another smoke.

"Naw. Thanks, man," said X. "I'm planning on running track this year."

"Yeah, right and I'm gonna fly," laughed O. D.

"And I'm gonna turn white. And if I was white I could still beat your slow butt running," chimed in an equally amused Chance.

X grabbed his crotch. "Hey, both y'all can get on this."

O. D. and Chance boomed again in laughter.

"Wha, wha, whatcha talking bout, man? I don't see a damn thang. Chance, you see anything?"

The two boys howled again and slapped one another five.

"Your mamas," mumbled X.

"My mama probably got more dick than you," blurted O. D., who too late realized he had just made a mistake.

"That don't surprise me none. Your mamma look like a damn man with that hairy ass Groucho Marx looking mustache sprouting on her upper lip," X spat back gleefully, only too glad to play the dozens of which he was a master.

O. D. looked at Chance hoping for a little assistance in this insult flinging challenge.

"Hey, O. D. don't be lookin' at me to have your back. My brother, if I was you I would be hauling it down to the store to pick up a few cans of Magic Shave for your old lady." Chance was already scooting off the cement steps when he hurled the insult, deftly changing allegiance. Before he could get the words "Magic Shave" out of his mouth good, O. D. charged and eventually chased him across the school yard.

Because Chance was gripped by a spasm of laughter, O. D. had him in a bear hug before he had gotten more than 10 yards from the school's steps.

However, the short dash had already cooled O. D.'s temper. Mercifully, he only squeezed half the air out of Chance's bird chest and then proceeded to simply screw a ham-sized fist in the small of his back.

"Okay, man be cool. You messin' up my rags." Chance coughed out the words.

"Punk, don't let me have to get on Jan, cause you know I knows all bout your bowlegged mammy," said O. D. still twisting his knuckles hard into Chance's back.

"Okay. Okay. Cool. Just let me go."

O. D. slowly opened the vise of his arms and Chance squirmed free, tears of laughter and a little pain forming in the corners of his eyes. He smoothed the front of his lemon yellow Alpaca sweater and pinched the crease in his pants, running his fingers down the front of both legs.

"Why don't you knuckleheads stop playing round?" complained Biggie as he strode up to his friends, even more pissed that he had been minutes before.

"Man, the show starts at 6. I don't know bout y'all but I say forget Roach. I ain't waiting another second for his rusty ass. I say we hat up right now." Biggie scanned the faces of his three friends for affirmation.

"Big, you know how Roach be. He be late to his own funeral. He said he be here round five or so and it's only. . ." O. D. looked down helplessly at his naked wrist.

"Five-twenty," said Chance, a look of concern now playing in his face. He didn't really want to side with Biggie and leave Roach behind, but it was getting late and he didn't want to miss a second of the Temptations and Jr. Walker at Leo's.

"Big is right. It's gonna take at least 30 minutes to get down to Leo's, and that's if the bus ain't late," continued Chance.

"That's what I'm sayin'. You know how Roach is. He could be off on another one of his explorations. And if that's the case, we might not see that fool for two or three days," Biggie noted, satisfied that he had persuaded his friends to his point of view.

They all knew Biggie was right. For as long as any of them could remember, at least as long as they had known Roach, he would just up and disappear, usually for hours but at least twice, for two days, with nobody, not even his parents, knowing where he had gone.

The first time Roach had disappeared was at the age of 7, at least that was the tale according to Mrs. Gouldsby, the widow lady who lived next door to Roach's family. Chance remembered his father calling Mrs. Gouldsby a busy body who had "a Ph. D. in dipping."

"That boy was just a little old thang, no more than 6 or 7 when he took it in his head to jump on that 48A bus that stops right in front of my house. Seven years old, up and gone and them Harris didn't even knowed he was missing. Now can you imagine such a thing," said Mrs. Gouldsby, pulling the edges of her red wig down on her head. She had stopped in to welcome the Marshalls to the neighborhood and to fill them in on all their neighbors as well to pick up any tidbits about the newest arrivals to Walden Avenue that she could. Chance hadn't planned on meeting Mrs. Gouldsby, but his mother had grabbed him and made him introduce himself.

"Please excuse my son. Sometimes he forgets his manners." The words were delivered with a hard pinch to Chance's upper arm.

Just as he was about ready to exit the room, right after telling Mrs. Gouldsby his age, to which the nosy widow woman replied—"My, my aren't we small for 10"—Chance halted in his tracks when she evoked Roach's name "That Lindsey Harris is 10. Chance is he in your class?"

But before Chance could respond, Mrs. Gouldsby had embarked on her story about Roach.

" That little Harris boy was all the way downtown. Police called that night around 10 said they found him wandering around the stadium. Don't you know that boy had snuck into a Indians baseball game."

Chance was just about to get comfortable and listen to the rest of the information the old woman was going to share about the boy he had just recently met, when his mother said, "Excuse me, young man. Can't you see that adults are holding a conversation? Tell, Mrs. Gouldsby it was nice meeting her, and you go out and play."

Chance only went as far as the kitchen. He sat out of sight behind the counter and strained his ears.

"Lawd, Mrs. Marshall. Can I call you Jan?" asked the widow woman without taking a breath as she snatched on her wig again. "Jan, them Harrises is no account. You know they both drink." She paused to gauge Mrs. Marshall's reaction to the news. Getting none she ploughed right back into her story.

"Well, anyway, because they was both drunk I had to drive down to the police station with Mr. Harris, smelling like booze, to pick up little Lindsey. It was all I could do to keep Mr. Harris in the car and not go into the police station.

"That was the first time he took off on his lonesome. Just a little old man that's what that Lindsey is. On the way back from the station the little fella said he had gotten tired of asking his father to take him to see the Indians play so he went by himself.

"I tell you that boy is some independent. But he got to be with folks like he got. I'm telling you it's Lindsey that raises those Harris kids, all five of them. He's the responsible adult in that household. That little old man. . ."

Chance smiled as he thought about Mrs. Gouldsby description of Roach "Little Old man."

In the four years since Chance first learned about Roach's treks, his friend had gone on at least a dozen other similar journeys, the most famous, as far as anyone knew, being the one he took to Buffalo two years ago when he was 13. That time he had gone to the Chester Avenue bus terminal and hopped a Greyhound bus which he took all the way to western New York state with plans of going to Canada to see the falls.

Chance had learned of that adventure from O. D., who had heard the story from his mother. Seems that the only reason Roach got off in Buffalo was because he got scared that he would be put in jail because he didn't have a passport. That time Mr. Harris had been sober enough to retrieve his son without the help of Mrs. Gouldsby. It was only weeks later that Roach discovered that he didn't need a passport and that he could have seen Niagara Falls from the American side.

Roach seldom, if ever, shared details about his adventures and when he did talk the information only came out in snippets and always in indirect ways.

However, Chance knew that at least one of Roach's favorite destinations was Lake Erie, more specifically the Goodtime sightseeing boat, which trolled the shore of the lake around the Ninth Street pier before heading up the Cuyahoga River and then back again.

Chance had come about the bit of intelligence last year when Mrs. McBeth, his 8th grade civics teacher, took his entire class on trip aboard the Goodtime. Roach, who sat next to him in that class and next to him that day on the boat, was greeted warmly by the Goodtime's captain. When Mrs. McBeth asked Roach how he had come to know the captain he just shrugged. Later, while they counted the dead fish floating on the river's thick coffee-colored waters as the boat slogged along down the twisting Cuyahoga, Roach told Chance that he had ridden the Goodtime at least a dozen times.

"I like coming down here because it's peaceful. I was coming so much old Captain Quinn started letting me on for free."

And that was that. Roach never said anything more on the subject.

"Chance. You coming or what?" The words startled Chance, who was lost in thought. When he finally gathered himself he was looking up into O. D.'s round moon face.

"Man, we ain't waiting for Roach no more," said O. D. jogging to catch up with Biggie and X, who were already halfway down the block.

"Hey, you all. You better hurry up, here come the bus."

Chance and O. D., responding to Biggie's warning, broke into a dead run.

White light exploded in a thousand shards off the chrome skin of the microphone as it sailed upward through the smokey blackness. The smoke wasn't really visible until it drifted into the narrow shaft of stark white light that tracked the microphone's ascent.

Something grabbed the mic's black tail, stopping its motion in midair. The silvery implement hung there in the waves of smoke and then tumbled back to earth. Its free fall was interrupted by a black hand that snatched the microphone. As soon as those long black fingers clamped around the microphone, choking the live wire in a ham fist, that shaft of light flashed off. For several seconds, that seem to stretch into minutes, everything was black and silent. The silence was shattered by a gravel on sandpaper wail.

"Iiiiiiiiii know you want to leave me but I refuse to let you go."

Light from twenty different directions flooded the room and focused on the five, tall, slick, white suited figures posing in the middle of the stage. The mahogany skin statues, who would have made the Greek god Adonis jealous, in unison broke out in a frenzy of slides, kicks, and twirls hands chopping, heads bobbing, fingers popping. The club pulsated with rhythms that rocketed up and down the spines of the audience crowded around small white skirted tables pushed up just inches from the stage.

"Damn, them Temps are some bad boys!"

"You ain't never lied X," said Biggie, draining his glass of R. C. Cola. Leo's Casino. It wasn't much more than a rough around the edges show bar several dozen tables squeezed in a dark, low ceilinged, black walled room, on the wrong side of town, but the place was magic.

Leo's was Mecca if your religion was at times hard-driving, back-bone bending beats and at other times, silky smooth, ear caressing rhythms of soul music. Leo's was where the biggest and brightest black stars in the entertainment universe held court-Marvin Gaye, Smokey and the Miracles, the Supremes, Wilson Picket, Flip Wilson, Mary Wells, Otis Redding, Dick Gregory, the O'Jays. Pimps, prostitutes, politicians and lawyers, white businessmen, ghetto hustlers, rosy cheeked suburban kids, glassy eyed street kids - Leo's is where they all came together, where they stood in line, pressed up against one another, position and pretense dropped, stood there in eager anticipation, stood there united in a common cause to pay homage to the kings and queens of soul.

"Well, well my brothers. I see that you made it." Chance turned in his seat and looked at the hand on his shoulder. He followed his eyes across the hand and then up the arm until they bumped into a beaming Roach.

"Man, where you been? Messin' round waiting for you and we missed Jr. Walker." The words rumbled out of Biggie low and mean.

"Sssh. Keep it down," whispered Roach easing into a vacant chair next to Chance. He scooted forward twice in the chair, the first time a leg was grabbed by a snag in the blood red carpet. Once situated, his bony elbows resting on the 18-inch wide square of table top, he offered an explanation of sorts.

"Look, I just had to split the pad early is all. I know I should've called one of y'all but I knew you wouldn't wait for me too long so I figured I just meet you down here."

"Lucky for you, chump, that your cousin remembered we was your boys and let us in for half price," Biggie continued scolding Roach.

"Like I said I knew y'all be here cause I got the hook-up." Roach said referring to his cousin as he puffed out his chest and held out an upturned palm in front of Chance.

"So it's going to be like that. You going to leave me hanging?" asked Roach looking at Chance, his palm still outstretched waiting to be skinned.

Reluctantly Chance slapped Roach's hand, snapping his fingers as soon as they had finished sliding across the boy's calloused palm.

"Damn, Roach, you could be a little more considerate," complained Chance.

"Well, consider that over there, my man." Roach nodded across the room at a table near the far end of the stage. Biggie and X had to shift around in their seats to see, but Chance immediately focused on the two white girls, both with straight, blond shoulder length hair that was curled up on the ends, alternately sipping on drinks and dancing in their seats.

"MmmmmMmm. Now, they're finer than a gnat's eyelash," crooned Roach, slicking down the sides of his conked head and licking his lips.

"Yeah, so what? They with them three white dudes. And they look like they in college anyway," Chance noted, turning his attention back to the stage.

"That don't mean nothin'. And look at them cats. They some real lames," observed Biggie, smiling fingering a piece of ice from his class. Sucking on the piece of ice, he continued.

"Betcha if I can get me some eye contact up in here them chicks gonna give me the number."

"Them broads ain't even thinkin' bout us," X yawned as he tipped up the napkin lined plastic basket on the table looking for some more potato chips. Since it was empty, he wetted an index finger and smeared it around the bottom of the basket and retrieved some crumbs.

"You and Roach always getting excited about some white tail," mumbled X, pulling the salty finger from his lips with a smack.

"Put a long blond wig on your yellow ass and you can be my ho," hissed Biggie.

"Why you two always got to be at each other? Just be cool and let's watch the show before you get us thrown out of here," Chance said, eyeing Biggie and X. It annoyed him that Biggie and X seem to always be bad mouthing each other, up in one another's face. Their beefs with one another seemed to always involve color, which didn't make much sense because they both were damn near white and seemed pretty much pleased with the fact.

"Check it out. Check it out," Roach whispered excitement in his voice. "I'm tellin' you them chickaboos are diggin' on us. Well, maybe not on us," he added, poking Chance in the ribs.

Chance told Roach to "jump in the lake." Still, he looked over at the girls hopefully. Damn if they weren't smiling at them, at least when they weren't holding their heads down, or glancing over at the guys at the table with them. When the blondes stood up and headed toward what Chance was sure were the restrooms near the back of the club, he urged Roach to get up and bump into them accidentally on purpose.

"Why me? Why don't you do it, Mister All Big and Bad," countered Roach.

"Both you two little fags. Let a man do the job," said Biggie, slowly rising from his chair and then posing.

"Yo, youngblood sit your monkeyass down or move out the way, you blockin my lady's view," said the black mountain of a man, his "lady" smiling sheepishly, her face pressed against his massive shoulder.

Chance and Roach sunk down in their chairs. X turned and looked at the man and then up at Biggie and smiled.

"No problem, brotha," was all Biggie was able to stammer as he cut his eyes at X and quickly moved away from the table. He stumbled slightly over the leg of his chair as he beat a hasty exit.

"Excuse me, ladies. Can I have your number cause I done forgot mine after diggin on you two," crooned Biggie as he saddled up to the blond girls, having regained his composure. He grinned a grin like a grill on a 57 Buick. Biggie plunked two quarters in the cigarette machine that separated the door to the men's john from the door to the ladies restroom but he never took his eyes or grin off of the girls.

One of the girls bent down to retrieve the pack of Winstons that slid across the machine's metal tray. She giggled as she handed them to Biggie.

"You going to the restroom or you going stand out here talking to this turkey?" asked a heavy set black woman rolling her eyes in disgust. She didn't wait for an answer and pushed by the group, giving Biggie a purposeful nudge.

"Brothers and white girls," she hissed under her breath as she brushed past and disappeared through the rest room door.

"Ouch," said Biggie in mock distress and then he laughed. "So which one of you lovely ladies will I have the pleasure of making their acquaintance first?"

"I'm Gloria and this is Tammy."

"Well, I'm Julian," said Biggie, reaching first to kiss the back of Gloria's hand.

"And they call me X and I'm the one you ladies really want to meet." Now it was Biggie's turn to roll his eyes.

X, matching the wattage of Biggie's grin tooth for tooth pressed on. "So how are you ladies diggin the show? He squeezed next to Tammy as another woman pushed by the foursome and into the restroom.

"The Temptations are the most. Really boss," said Tammy, feeling a little less nervous.

X and Biggie looked at one another and fought back their laughter.

"So, like who you two down here with?" coughed Biggie through a stifled chuckle. "Tammy's older brother and two of his college roommates," said Gloria, brushing a stray strand of hair out of her blue eyes, which were made even more blue thanks to the smudge of violet eye shadow over her heavy lids.

"Do you go to college?" X asked.

"Me and Tammy? No." Both girls giggled and Tammy blushed.

"We're juniors at Beachwood High," continued Gloria.

"You could have sure fooled us. The way you carry yourselves and everything, I could have sworn you two were 20, 22." Biggie tried his best to sound sincere.

There was a silence that hung between the four for a long couple of seconds when Tammy piped up.

"Well, I guess we better be getting back to our table before we're missed."

"Too late," broke in Gloria, heaving out an exasperated sigh.

Tammy, X, and Biggie looked in the direction of Gloria's stare.

"Damn, it's my brother and Lenny. We better get on into the restroom, Gloria."

X reached out and gently caught Tammy by the hand.

"You can't just run off like that. Don't you have any respect for a man's heart?" X made it a point to continue holding Tammy's hand in his.

"Hey, Lenny. Hey, David," blurted Gloria, much too loudly. The boys looked at X and Biggie and then at the two girls.

"Lenny. David. Great show, isn't it guys? Aren't the Temptations simply boss?" X did his best white boy voice imitation, and held Tammy's hand with both of his and grinned but his eyes weren't smiling.

The white boys stared for a second or two and then pushed through the door marked Men.

Turning to the girls, "they seem like real neat guys, don't you agree Julian?" asked X.

"Well, I think we better get on back to the table," said Tammy, slipping her hand from X's grip and tugging on the bottom of Gloria's yellow miniskirt.

"So where are you heading after the show? The Red Carpet Lounge is nice if you want to do some dancing," said Biggie to Gloria, who really wasn't in the mood to head back to her table.

"You and Gloria should see if you can talk your brother and Lenny, and the other cat, into taking you down there after the show. It just a few blocks away," said X.

Tammy yanked on Gloria's dress again. "We'll ask them, but I'm sure they won't want to go." said Tammy. "Gloria, come on."

"Gloria, do you have a piece of paper or something?" asked Biggie, pulling an ink pen from his shirt pocket.

Gloria rummaged through her tiny hand bag, which couldn't have held more than a compact and a lipstick.

"Come on, Gloria," said Tammy, shifting from foot to foot as she looked at the men's bathroom door.

"Here give me your hand," commanded Gloria, taking the pen from Biggie. When Biggie stuck out his hand she grabbed it and turned it palm up. Slowly she scribbled her phone number in Biggie's hand. While she wrote, she stole glances at the men's room.

Tammy couldn't handle the tension anymore and started to walk away.

"Call me tomorrow, okay?" asked Gloria as she scurried to catch up with Tammy. When she was just a few steps away she realized that she had Biggie's pen and started to return.

Biggie waved her off and indicated that she should keep the pen.

"Call me," mouthed Gloria.

X and Biggie watched approvingly as the two girls shimmied away.

"Check it out," said Biggie elbowing X in the side.

Lenny and David stepped out of the restroom both with sour looks plastered on their faces.

X bore his eyes hard on them as he fixed a phony smile on his face.

"Hope you guys enjoy the rest of the show," X said in a tone much louder than needed.

X and Biggie watched approvingly as Lenny and David stalked away.

Once back at the table Biggie showed off his phone number, holding it close to the candle on the table so Roach and Chance could read it better.

Both Roach and Chance were upset that they hadn't approached the girls and for the rest of the night looked longingly across at them. Biggie made it a point that Gloria saw him slip his hand inside his shirt next to his heart a gesture that made Gloria bring her hand to he face to cover her smile.

X eyed Lenny and David and smiled every time their eyes met.

"Like a snowball rolling down the side of a snow covered hill, it's growing. Like the size of the fish the fisherman says broke his reel. It's growing. . . ."

X, Biggie, O. D., Roach and Chance sang at the top of their lungs. Mimicking the dance moves of the Temptations as they sang. They headed out of Leo's, through the throng that had gathered waiting to get in the 10 o'clock show and headed down the street.

"You see them chicks come out?" asked Biggie, looking back toward Leo's.

"Don't think they came out yet," said O. D. also spying the club's entrance.

Roach stopped at the bus stop less than 100 feet from Leo's.

"Man, what you doing?" asked Biggie.

"What it look like? Waiting for the bus."

"We can't be catching the bus this close to Leo's. What if somebody sees us," complained Biggie.

"You mean what if them two white babes see us," added O. D.

"Well, they can sure enough see me cause I ain't told them I'm in college," laughed Roach.

"I'm with Roach. I ain't walking a couple blocks just so them broads won't see us catching the bus. But we can go across the street and wait awhile till after they gone then catch the bus," Chance suggested.

"Well, if y'all gonna stand around and wait, I'm going down to Peter Pan and get me some donuts," said O. D., counting the change in his pocket determining how many donuts he could buy.

"Anybody, coming with me?" asked O. D.

"I'll go if you loan me a buck," said Roach.

O. D. really didn't want to give up a dollar; it meant, four less donuts for him. But he also didn't want to walk the four blocks to Peter Pan alone. Not that he was fearful, he just wanted some company.

"Well, we will wait over there across the street until y'all get back," said X. O. D. and Roach headed down Euclid while X, Chance and Biggie crossed.

The trio waded into the heavy traffic, which had slowed in front of Leo's, with people getting out of cars. A couple of cars stopped in the middle of the street holding conversations and still others just slowed down to see who they could see in front of the club.

Chance, X, and Big went down a side street lined with cars, most of them belonging to folks who were going to Leo's.

"I love that place," said Chance, soaking in the energy thrown off by the lights and people in front of Leo's.

"I wonder how much loot that place pull in on the weekend? I betcha whoever own that joint is rolling in the dough," Biggie speculated.

"Speaking of dough, I wish I had given O. D. some money to bring me back a few of them honey glazed. I'm getting hungry," said X.

"Man, forget them sweets. When we get in the neighborhood, I'm heading down to Whitmores and cop me a shoulder dinner, with extra sauce," announced Chance.

"You going to get off five blocks before our stop for some Bar-B-Que? Why don't you go right down the street to Hot Sauce Williams?" quizzed X.

" Cause your ass already said you were starving. You ain't got no money.

And I ain't sharing," said Chance.

"Chance, you cold," said X, throwing a couple playful jabs at his friend.

"Hey, what they up to?" asked Biggie. Chance and X stopped slap boxing and looked across the street at a white man leaning inside a cop cruiser clearly engaged in conversation. Several times the white man, probably in his late 30s or early 40s, pointed in their direction.

When he finished talking he stepped up onto the curb and wrapped his arm around a woman, most likely his wife, and walked back through Leo's front doors.

The cop car made a slow arcing turn. The cherry light on top of the cruiser flashed silently, stopping the traffic in both directions. The trio watched as the cruiser purred as it slowly approached.

"What you boys doing out here?" asked the cop on the passenger side, fitting his blue cap onto his head of red hair as he waited for an answer.

"Just waiting for a bus, that's all," replied Chance.

"So why you waiting here? The bus stop is across the street."

"We just came out of the show and we were waiting for a couple of friends to get back from the donut shop." Biggie answered the officer's question this time.

"Show has been out for 20 minutes now and in that time three buses have passed. You boys sure you ain't breaking into cars?"

"Oh, no way, officer. Like I said sir, we just waiting for a couple friends to get back," continued Biggie.

"And them weren't the bus we were waiting for," said X in a very matter of fact tone, which the one police officer picked up on.

Chance quickly added, "We're waiting on the 48A. That one stops on our block."

"Look here, boys. I want you guys on the very next bus that comes by. I don't care if it's the 48 A, the 32 D, the 55 Z., or the 99x. I don't give a damn where it's going. I want you on it. Or you three can take a little ride with me and my partner and I guarantee you won't like where we will take you."

Chance could hear the police man behind the wheel give a low chuckle.

"What about our friends?" Biggie asked.

"What about them? They big boys just like you. They can find their way home. Ain't that right, Officer Sturvoc?"

"Affirmative," replied the driver.

"Matter of fact, I think we better escort these boys. Make sure they get to the bus stop safely."

Turning from his partner and looking back out the open window at Chance, X, and Biggie, the red-headed policeman ordered "Let's get to stepping boys." He banged a flat palm twice on the roof of his black and white.

Chance, X, and Biggie crossed the street and walked silently up Euclid to the bus stop, the cop car shadowing their steps.

CHAPTER 7

THE RAIN OF SALTY SWEAT THAT POURED down O. D.'s face in a dozen tiny rivers and broke off in a hundred different directions as they flowed off his high round forehead didn't seem to phase him.

Some of the snaking trickles of sweat traced down the sides of his head, dipping into the cave of his ears and out again down the boy's thick neck. It was a neck that was solidly buttressed by two rows of flesh, stacked like two worn tires, which bulged in the squat space between his heavy shoulders and the base of his massive, perfectly round skull.

The other tributaries of perspiration rolled down the bridge of O. D.'s great flat nose, following the equally flat contours of his moon face. The sweat fanned out over the ledge stretching to both coasts of his face. If eyebrows had covered the ridge of flesh, even just a hint of hair, the sweat wouldn't have flowed unabated into O. D.'s eyes. Yet, the sting of sweat had no effect. O.D.'s eyes refused to blink.

Chance stared back into those determined eyes as they tracked his movements.

Going up against O. D. was a challenge that Chance relished, although he had to admit to himself, he preferred having the big man on his team, which was usually the case.

Before Chance and O. D. had finally earned the right to play round ball at the Mount, the two friends had battled one-on-one in each other's backyards for years. Chance pitting his quickness and agility against O. D.'s weight and height advantage, which had only increased over the years.

At 15, just a year older than Chance, O. D. was what the old folks called "full growed." At 6'-1 and 200 pounds, O. D. had Chance by four inches and a good 90 pounds.

As Chance bounced the slick leather ball from his right hand to his left and back again, he chewed on the word "spunk" as he mentally steeled himself to make a move.

Spunkanacity. That was the exact word O. D. had coined to describe Chance's determination during their countless basketball skirmishes.

Spunkanacity. The word had always pissed Chance off, throwing salt into the psyche wounds he suffered every time O. D. beat him and O. D. knew it, too. Still, O. D. admired Chance, although he would never tell him so, for the way his friend had never given up and fought to the end of every one of their round ball contests no matter how lopsided the score would get. Their backyard battles, that often resembled wrestling matches, had sharpened both of their skills, making them the first of the "youngbloods" to be given the right to play in the games at the Mount.

The Mount, the cracked asphalt courts at Gracemount Elementary School that had to be swept clear of broken glass, were reserved for the serious basketball players of the neighborhood, hoopsters who considered themselves the equals of Dave Bing, Elgin Baylor, Wilt, and the Big O-Oscar Robertson.

Chance and O. D. had practically lived at the Mount for the last three years, mainly watching and anxiously hoping from the sidelines. They didn't hold out much hope of being picked for a game, so they appeased themselves with bouncing balls on the sidelines and providing play-by-play commentary with appropriate, "ohs", "and", ahs. During the short breaks between games as the winners ambled to the water fountain, and the guy with "next" selected his team, O. D., Chance and the rest of the sideline regulars, who lined the squat metal rail that separated the school parking lot from the playground, scurried like roaches onto the court. They put on dribbling and shooting exhibitions, hoping that a 360-spin move to the basket, or a half court rainbow jumper, or a between the legs, behind the back move would get them noticed by the "playas".

After years of being passed over when sides were picked, O. D., almost fainted when a year ago, at the age of 14 he was selected to run.

He was so shocked that he stood motionless and had to be pushed in. He was shaky, but when he drove the lane taking Garland Jones, one of the legends of Mount to the hole, he was officially in and in for good.

O. D. rubbed it in that he had become a player and his running buddies, especially Chance, had not. Fortunately for Chance's ego O. D.'s bragging was short lived; Chance was finally plucked from the sidelines just three months after O. D.'s debut. Sure, Chance had gotten in on a humble, when Gacy Farley twisted his ankle and had to go to the sidelines. That day it had been raining off and on so that the usual contingent of railbirds had been significantly whittled down. As matter of fact it was only Chance and Bubby and Tony, 10 year old twins, who had also braved the elements on that particular day.

But once Chance had gotten the taste of the big time, he was determined never to rejoin the ranks of the rail sitters.

Spunkanacity. That's how O. D. chalked up Chance's surprising graduation to the big time. In short order, Biggie, Roach and X joined O. D. and Chance in holding sway at the Mount.

"Whatcha got, boy?" growled O. D., waving at Chance to bring it on.

Dribbling in place, Chance gave a little juke of his head on every third bounce of the ball, one time to the right, the other to the left, waiting for O. D. to bite on the fake.

O. D., with arms outstretched simply danced on the balls of his feet, taking in deep controlled gulps of oxygen as he kept Chance fixed square in his sight.

"Pass the rock, man!"

Chance was only half aware of the call that came from somewhere behind him. But it wouldn't had mattered if the voice had been connected to a body standing right next to him and that body happened to belong to Bing, Elgin or the Big O, Chance wouldn't have passed the ball. He was determined to take O. D. to the hole.

If it had been Roach, or Biggie or even X guarding Chance, he might have considered passing the ball to an open teammate, who would have to be standing totally unguarded underneath the basket, maybe. But this was O. D., and he wasn't going to loose face giving up the rock.

O. D. knew it, too, although he didn't take their rivalry nearly as seriously as Chance. But that didn't mean that he wasn't firm in his determination to stop Chance cold.

Wiping his hands on his shirt, O. D. crouched slight over and hiked up his pants, until the cuffs reached just below his calves.

"Damn, he always do that shit," growled Roach throwing up his hands and shaking his head completely disgusted.

Chance looked in Roach's direction and noticed that Biggie had joined his teammate in their disillusionment. Both were relegated to spectator status as they watched the battle between Chance and O. D. unfold.

Picking up the pace of his dribble, Chance moved to his right in an abbreviated skipping motion, the ball thudding at his side as his glided toward the right corner of the court. O. D. shadowed his movements.

Then with a sudden burst Chance flung the basketball between his legs and into his left hand, pivoted on his sneakers, the rubber soles squealing at the rapid change in direction, and darted full tilt to his left and across the lane.

O. D. wasn't fooled and was on Chance like white on rice. Both boys were just inches apart, the heat from their bodies colliding. With his free hand Chance slapped at O. D.'s right arm, which he had stuck in the small of his back.

They were both moving at almost a dead run, a foot race to the basket. But just as suddenly as he had exploded to his left, Chance braked to a stop. He had hoped O. D.'s momentum would have continued taking him toward the basket. All Chance wanted was a little bit of separation, four or five inches, just enough space between them to launch a jumper.

"Fade away in your face, chump!" The words sprung from Chance's mouth just as his feet lifted off the black top. His arms were bent above his head, the ball rested on just the tips of his fingers and his left wrist was cocked back in firing position.

The clear look at the basket Chance had when he reached the apex of his leap was blotted out just as he released the ball.

O. D.'s catcher's mitt of a hand rocketed into Chance's field of vision. Almost simultaneously a sound that reminded Chance of the thud the pumpkins had made when he and his brother's had snuck into Old Lady Gouldsby's garden a couple of years ago and smashed the orange gourds, filled his ears.

"Wham!" The flat of O. D.'s fat hand slapped the basketball back over Chance's head.

One of O. D.'s teammates picked up the loose ball and nonchalantly dribbled to the opposite basket and laid it in. Roach and Biggie offered no challenge and simply looked on in continued disgust as the boy scored the winning basket.

"As long as you is black, don't never bring no weak stuff up in here, boy," said O. D., balling up his fists and landing a stiff one-two-combination into the air.

"That's game, ain't it Chance? Y'all kept it close, hey, but what can I say 'cept, get the hell off the court so I can get me some real com-poe-tit-shun!" O. D. chuckled deeply and stuck out his hand.

"Go to hell!"

"Chance, my man, you ain't gonna to slap me five on that? Wow, yous ah hard brotha. But you got spunkanacity. That's what I like bout you boy." This time O. D. wrapped Chance in a playful bear hug.

"Get off me, O. D." Chance was hot and pushed hard at O. D., but he knew he wasn't breaking free until O. D. decided to release him.

"You know you still my boy," said O. D., letting Chance go.

"Next!" O. D. bellowed.

Several figures raced pass Chance toward the court, but he didn't notice them as he shuffled, head down to the sideline.

"Damn, you don't never pass," scolded Roach as he sauntered up next to Chance.

"You always ball hogging. Hell, I was wide open."

"Shut up, Roach. You would have thrown up a brick anyway," Chance spat back.

"Yeah, like getting the ball smacked back in your face is any better."

"Just shut up, Roach and call winnas."

"Already did. And you can bet I ain't pickin' your ball hogging ass to run wid me."

"Go to hell, Roach."

"Naw, you go sit your non-playin' butt on the sidelines chump," Roach shot back, laughing and slapping five to a group of boys sitting on the guard rail framing the parking lot.

Chance moved to the far end of the guardrail, which had been carefully bent, its top folded down toward the ground to form something like a bench, which offered just about four inches of surface to sit on. Plopping down he took off his wet T-shirt and mopped the sweat first from his face and then from under his arms. As he wiped the soggy shirt over his chest, Biggie joined him on the rail.

"Don't come over here starting with me. I lost the game, alright?" Chance sighed. He rubbed at his arm pits one more time before resting his elbows on his thighs and hanging his head, his fatigue made up of equal parts exhaustion and humiliation.

"Man, you gots me wrong. I just came over to talk to Wig."

"Huh?" Chance looked up questioningly at Biggie. The yellow skinned boy nodded his freckled face toward the far end of the parking lot. They both watched in silence as the sunrise yellow Cadillac crept, cat-like into the parking lot, its gold-plated front bumper raising slightly as the car's front wheels bounced over the elevated lip of the driveway.

Chance and Biggie got up from their perch and moved toward the Caddy. Roach fell in behind them.

As they walked Chance smoothed his hair, the wet strands forming rows of waves under the press of his palms. He snatched a stocking cap from his back pocket and pulled it tight over his skull.

Biggie subconsciously pawed at the sides and back of his head and to himself, cursed his naps and Chance. "It wasn't fair that a dark nigger like

Chance would have good hair and someone as light as himself had to tussle with buckshot," Biggie thought, moving his palm over the knots on his head. Biggie swore that he was going to finally get his hair conked and damn what his mother had to say.

As the boys approached, the back windows of the car drifted down in a smooth mechanical motion and the rear driver's side door swung open.

The first thing that appeared was a red high heel shoe and then a long, shapely white leg. When the girl finally got around to twisting the rest of her ample, but very sexy body out of the car, all eyes were on her. She hopped on one foot, balancing herself on the car's door, as she screwed the other high heel shoe onto her bare foot.

Establishing that the shoe was firmly in place, by stamping her foot on the ground twice, she proceeded to tug at the bottom of her hot-pink miniskirt, which no matter how hard she pulled, wasn't even thinking about reaching the middle of her thick pale thighs.

Flipping back the mop of blond hair out of her eyes, the white girl looked at the boys and smiled and then pushed a pair of oversized sunglasses, the oval lenses as big as the bottoms of coffee mugs, up her long, straight, freckled-nose.

"Well, bitch, you gonna open my door or what?" The question squeezed out of the opening at the top of the driver's front door, its window cracked open less than an inch.

Startled, the white girl wiggled to the front door and pulled on the gold plated handle, breaking a nail in her rush.

When the door yawned open, the girl retreated quickly to the rear of the car, removed her shoes so not to scratch the high-gloss paint job, and pulled herself up onto the trunk.

The rear of the yellow Caddy sunk down as the driver stepped from the car.

"Hoes. Hoes got to be told what to do. A man that lets a hoe think for herself ain't gonna have nothing but the trouble his sorry ass deserves."

Wig paused to let his words sink in. For as long as Chance had known Wig, he had never started a conversation with a greeting or an acknowledgment to those he addressed. And it didn't matter if there were other conversations going on when he arrived on the scene. Wig just went right into his speech, figuring what he had to say took precedent over all other conversations. When it came to Chance and his friends, Wig had figured right.

Leaning his lanky body back against the gold-plated front grill of his Caddy, Wig took a long, deep drag, sucking the last of the orange life from his Kool cigarette.

"You young boys be wanting to wine and dine and romance these bitches."

Wig's words came in short blasts of menthol smoke as he flicked the cigarette stub across the parking lot.

"Buying broads a bunch of shit, being all polite is fine for punks who want some bitch shaking his pockets. And, believe me, that's exactly what will happen to your lame asses if you come that way with a chick."

Wig, regal in an iridescent lime green shark skin suit, was holding court.

A snap from his manicured fingers, which looked like sticks dipped in black lacquer, jerked up the blond mop of hair from the trunk of the Caddy.

The mop eased a just lit cigarette from the smeared red crease that sat where her mouth should have been.

Sliding like melted butter down the sunbaked trunk and between the Caddy's rear fins, the mop gingerly pranced on red-painted toes across the lot's molten asphalt to give Wig the rest of her smoke.

The white girl carefully inserted the brown filter between his huge, fleshy, blue-black lips. Wig didn't acknowledge her presence. He blew out a cloud of smoke, and continued his train of thought.

"A hoe wants a man to run the show. She wants a man to be the whole show."

When he spoke, Wig used his entire body, what little there was of it, on his six-foot frame. His mean thin hands, topped by long fingers that started at his wrists, sliced the air in quick, short Judo chops to emphasis the words he hissed through the gaps of his teeth.

Wig's wide expanse of pock-marked ebony face, that bobbed and weaved on a broom handle neck, was wildly animated. Yellow slits, that passed for eyes, darted from side to side under the ever undulating waves of his shiny, furrowed brow.

But Wig's most impressive feature was a flat broad nose, which spread out toward his ears at the opposite coasts of his black face. It was a nose that when crunched tight in a wrinkled sneer, snorting billows of menthol smoke, as it often did, announced boldly that its owner was not a man to be messed with.

Wig's nose was unusually passive this afternoon. The sea on his forehead was equally calm and placid.

Like he did most summer afternoons, Wig had stopped by the basketball court behind Gracemount School, the Mount, to watch a little round ball and to "school you fag ass young bloods."

This was exactly why Chance hadn't wanted to go to Florida this summer. He had missed out on too many of Wig's lectures on life, while he was stuck in the country South.

Last summer, at least according to Biggie, Wig had let him get a freebie from one of his girls. Although nobody else had verified Biggie's story. Of course, none of them was brave enough to ask Wig if Biggie was lying or not.

Still, the truth of the matter was that just hanging around Wig and smiling at his girls made Chance feel like a man.

"Y'all need educating bad. Hell, y'all won't make it out here in da streets if you don't start digging what Wig be trying to tell you."

To a bunch of dumb ass young boys, wanting so badly to be cool, needing so much to be "men," Wig, with his processed do, I-talian suits, alligator shoes, and diamond rings, was the real deal. Wig was the truth.

Wig was nothing like their daddies. He wasn't living a middle class, do the right thing, got to be twice as good, button down, credit to his race, responsible Negro life.

Wig was a Mack. A "you can kiss the crack of my rusty black ass muthafucka" type of cat. Wig was a pimp with a bunch of fine hoes and even more R-E-S-P-E-C-T.

Wig was too fly.

Well, at least as fly as one could be hustling in the very middle-class Negro confines of the Lee Harvard neighborhood.

Of course a bunch of dumb young asses didn't know that the hard core pimps who ran the Five, which was the hip name for East 105th Street down the way, would have had Wig's skinny, jive talking black ass turning tricks for them had they known he had the nerve to equate his jake flake hustle to pimping.

Hell, the only reason Wig hung out at the Mount's basketball court during the afternoons was because he worked the third shift at United Parcel where he loaded trucks, the only pay he could count on.

Still, Chance and his friends, who were so dumb that they would have a hard time figuring out how to get wet in the rain, stood in awe of Wig. O. D., Chance, Biggie, Roach and X, were the typical dumb middle-class colored boys trying their damnedest to be cool, to be players, so it was easy for someone like Wig to run game on them.

Yet and still, it was a smooth game, at least as far as they were concerned. Wig always had some fine young broads curled up in his ride, and not just Negro babes, but white girls—white girls like the one who just slid him the Kool.

"Peggy. Come here and sit with your daddy," Wig cooed at the blond mop.

Again the boys watched wide-eyed waiting for the white girl to again twist herself out of the back seat of the Caddy.

"Why the hell did you get back in my ride? You know your pale ass needs to be out here gettin all the sun you can. All that white skin makes you look sickly," barked Wig, the sticky sweetness gone from his voice.

Peggy's pale blue, crossed eyes, grew wide. She nearly wasted the pink polish she was applying in thick strokes, to her stubby chipped nails.

Peggy always had a hard time gauging Wig's moods. It wasn't that she was slow, as much as she was often in her own world.

But Wig's rough tone quickly brought her back to earth. All she knew was that the last thing she wanted was to get on his ugly side, which she understood was all too easy to do.

"Peggy! Don't let me haveta call your ass again girl."

"I'm coming, Daddy. Just let me get my shoes back on."

"Fuck them damn shoes and get you honky ass out here, now."

Wig flashed a stingy grin that barely turned up the corners of his fat purple lips, in the boys' direction.

The plump white girl looked to her two black companions for help.

Inez dismissed Peggy with a cut of her eyes, heavy with blue shadow.

Peach just ignored the white girl like she always did.

Timidly, Peggy scooted across the car's brown leather rear seat, stepped out the back door and padded sheepishly across the heated black top.

Twice without success, Peggy tried to slide her wide round hips, ass first, onto the Caddy's front fender. On her third attempt she searched for something to grip so she could pull herself up more easily.

"I tell you what, bitch, if you pull off my mirror I'll shonuff going to get all in your ass."

Peggy snatched her half-painted fingers away from the side mirror and quickly waddled around to the front of the car. Not sure of what to do next she stood still and stared at the ground not wanting to look into Wig's yellow slits.

At that moment it was impossible to tell if the repeated hollow thud came from the basketball, that X bounced between his skinny legs, or from Peggy's heart, as it frantically lifted and dropped her big freckled tits.

"My dear. May I be of assistance?" purred Wig extending a bony hand.

Peggy breathed again.

Smiling faintly, she took Wig's outstretched palm in hers, placed one barefoot on the gold-plated bumper and wiggled herself onto the Caddy's hood, resting her bare pink back on the welcome coolness of the car's windshield.

"Like I was saying little bros. A hoe wants a man to run the show. A man always takes control of the situation, he leads a bitch in the direction he wants her to go," said Wig patting at his pockets.

"Damn, I'm out of squares." Wig shot a low, mean look at Peggy.

Chance knew he shouldn't, but he couldn't help but to feel sorry for the white girl.

Panic flashed in her reddened face and all she could manage was a feeble shrug of her bare shoulders.

"Yo, Wig, I got some smokes," offered Roach bending to pull a green and white cellophane package of cigarettes wedged just inside the top of his high-top Chuck Taylor sneakers.

"Hey. Hey. Woo. Hold up my man. Whatcha doing? I don't want no damn smoke that's been in your damn funky tennis shoe. I mean, what the fuck is goin on here? Don't I got three hoes?" Wig screamed the words sending a spray of spit in all directions.

The panic that had filled Peggy's crossed eyes was now reflected in the eyes of the two black girls inside the Caddy.

"Baby, I'm fresh out," stammered Inez as she fumbled through her purse.

Whenever Inez was nervous, she fiddled in her hair. At this moment she was petrified.

Her pudgy fingers pulled and twisted at the platinum wig framing her tan, full moon face. Even though Inez was filled with fear, she was still conscious of being careful not to tug the wig so hard that it revealed the black buckshot at the back of her neck.

Peaches, a flat chested girl with a large gold tooth in the front of her mouth, which seem to be in a constant battle with her puffy lips, simply shrugged. She knew it was always safer to keep silent at times like these.

"Damn bitches ain't worth shit. If they were dying of thrist I wouldn't give them a sip of my pee.

"God Damnit, get your funky asses out of my ride and go get me some Goddamn smokes. Now. Damnit!"

"You mean all of us, daddy?" asked Inez.

"Whatcha think? Your big ass too special to hump to the store for me?"

"No baby. I was just wondering if. . ."

"SHUT THE FUCK UP!" Wigs' words came like a back hand, slapping the rest of Inez's thought down her throat.

Inez and the gold-tooth girl scrambled to get out of the car. Inez almost toppled over as she struggled to balance herself on one tree trunk leg, while trying to stuff a foot into a high heel. She broke her fall by catching Peggy by the shoulder, who had shot from the El's hood.

Peggy yanked at the back of her miniskirt, which seemed determined to ride up the back of her sunburned thighs to show off the roundness of her full hips and switched out of the parking lot.

Inez hopped, skipped, stumbled along beside the white girl, still unable to secure both shoes to her feet. But, the last thing Inez wanted to do was to stop moving.

The Tooth followed behind them.

"Yo."

That one syllable froze the trio in their spiked heel tracks.

"Take this," growled Wig, peeling a twenty from the wad of green clamped in his fist.

The Tooth shuffled over on bandy legs and cautiously stooped, so as not to rip her orange hot pants that she must have been poured into, to retrieve the bill Wig had tossed to the ground.

"Bring back a taste for me and my boys. Some Bird and some Rose."

"And some Bali High," blurted out Biggie before he had realized what he was saying.

The world screeched to a halt. Mouths fell open, even Wig's.

"I mean if its alright with you Wig. I, I, I, was just suggesting, er, I mean, ah, just asking, wondering maybe if it was cool with you."

Biggie tried to regroup but was blowing it.

"Whatcha standing round for. You heard the man. Bring him back some Bali High. And don't forget my change."

Wig was big enough to be merciful.

The other boys shot looks at Biggie that shouted "dumb ass." Biggie was not dumb, he knew full well how close he had come and how lucky he was.

The crisis over, the boys locked their gaze on the wonder of wide, round, juicy ass being flung from side to side to the staccato click of spiked heels as the trio headed down the street.

Wig leaned against the hog, a wide, white, gap-toothed tooth grin winched back the heavy purple lips. He was proud of his hoes and what his ownership of their bodies and minds said about him.

"You punks stop slobbering all over my women. Look at y'all, dicks poking out all over the place. Sorry muthafuckas. Play some ball and get your minds off of what you can't afford."

It wasn't pussy so much that was on the boy's minds. What they wanted is exactly what Wig possessed unchallenged, total control over women.

Wig snatched the ball from Biggie and slammed it hard against the blacktop, while fixing a long yellow stare on the pale faced teen.

"Fast break," yelled Wig, lofting the ball in a high arc down the court.

"I got twenty on my man Big and his team," announced Wig, slicking back the sides of his process between his palms.

It was game point, with Biggie's team up by two when Wig's women made it back.

"In your face, chump."

The 20-foot shot from the corner snapped the bottom of the tattered net that dangled from the front of the rusted rim.

"That's GAME baby," shouted X, his hand still cocked in a shooting position.

Sweaty, funky, chests heaved, sucking in air. Their owners, bent over with hands on knobby knees, waited impatiently to down the cool liquid that was snatched from chalky, pursed lips in mid-swallow.

"Damn man," coughed X, wiping the sticky wine dribbling down his chin with the back of his arm and looking up at Biggie, who now held the bottle X had been sipping from.

"Who knows where your lips have been white folks. You could have been munching at the Y last night," hissed Biggie. He didn't like X and took every opportunity to crack on his light skin even though he and X were about the same color. The difference was X had good hair that laid in slick rolling waves on top of his head, mocking the thatch of naps fused to Biggie's skull.

"I told you not to call me that," said X, a blue vein tensing at his temple.

Biggie ignored him, wiped the mouth of bottle with the tail of his shirt and sucked deep from the bottle.

"All you fags besta learn to eat some pussy like them white boys cause that will be the only way you tiny dick niggas will ever turn out a broad," sneered Wig, gyrating his narrow hips in wide sweeping circles.

"You boys ain't got what I got. Ain't that right, ladies?"

"You know it sweet daddy. You sure can work that thang," purred Peggy, pressing her thighs against Wig and dipping her hand to his crotch.

The Tooth rolled her eyes at the white girl and slid up on the other side of Wig.

Rearranging her wig in the rearview mirror, Inez didn't take notice of her sisters as they sandwiched Wig.

Peggy nuzzled a freckled cheek against Wigs face and plunged a pink tongue into the darkness of his ear as she rolled her belly across the zipper of his pants.

The Tooth toyed with the beads of black hair on Wig's chest, but she knew she had been outflanked by Peggy.

Wig paid no attention to either girl. Instead he threw back his large head, closed his yellow eyes, and turned up the bottle of Rose.

"Lawdy, Lawdy. I'm sweet peter jeter the shonuff womb beater," laughed Wig, pulling the bottle out of his huge purple mouth and replacing its coolness with Peggy's hot lips.

The Tooth, having been dismissed, slid the Rose from Wig's skeletal hand.

Suddenly, the playground fell dead silent and held its breath.

Wig stood in amazement as he watched the flat-chested black girl and his bottle.

Somehow, Peggy found the good sense to ease up off of Wig and move towards the Caddy's slowly closing rear door.

The Tooth was oblivious to what was going on around her. She was only thinking about how much she hated that white girl and how good and cool the wine tasted.

"WHAM!"

The slap came like a shotgun explosion. Crystalline shards of glass and cold wine sprayed out across bare legs.

The Tooth sat with her legs splayed wide on the glass speckled black top. A breast had jumped from her twisted tank top. Her glazed eyes were as big as the Caddy's headlights. A trickle of crimson bubbled from the corners of her wide open mouth.

"Bitch, who told you to put your dick-sucking lips on my wine? Is you out of your damn mind?"

Wig wasn't waiting for an answer. Instead he laid into the Tooth again with another gangster slap. Cupping her sobbing face in the vice of his mean, thin, hands, Wig kneeled and place his angry flat nose to hers.

"Don't you ever, as long as you is black, worthless and ugly touch anything you even think might belong to me. You understand me bitch. . . WELL, DO YOU?"

The Tooth frantically moved her mouth but nothing came out.

"Answer me bitch!" Wig sprayed her face with spit.

Again the Tooth tried to respond, but all she could manage were deep whimpers and a froth of tears and blood.

"Get your stanky ass out of my sight!"

The Tooth, too shaken to stand, crawled toward the Caddy's closed rear doors.

"Did I say for you to get in my ride?"

Not daring to look up, she shook her head - No.

"Go out and earn me some money! Damnit, all of you get the fuck out of my car and get me some cash," screamed Wig, jerking open the car's door.

Peggy and Inez tumbled out, scampered over the Tooth and made a hasty dash across the parking lot.

"Bitch got blood on my shirt. This shit ain't gointo come out. Fuck!"

As Wig dabbed at the tiny red spots on the front of his shirt with a silk handkerchief he slowly started to calm down.

"That's what I mean 'bout keeping hoes in line. A man gots to always be in control," said Wig not looking up from his shirt.

Wig closely inspected his suit to make sure the Tooth, who had crawled across the street, hadn't splattered on that, too.

"Crazy hoes," Wig mumbled and then broke out in a roar of laughter.

"Damn, these bitches sure make a man work," said Wig, resuming his professorial demeanor.

Wigs laughter was the cue for the playground to breathe again.

"You see that shit, Biggie? The next time you call me "white folks" I'm going to smack you like a bitch. Wham," woofed X, back handing the air and bouncing on his toes.

"You're the only hoe I sees round here," Biggie fired back.

"Your Mama," crowed X to a chorus of laughter.

The Mount had returned to a state of normalcy.

Wig eased behind the wheel of the Caddy and inspected his do in the mirror.

Wig turned the ignition key. The Marvelettes moaned from the radio *"My baby must be a magician cus he sure got the magic touch. . ."*

Slouched down and leaning to the right, Wig swung the Hog in a slow wide arc and eased out into the street.

CHAPTER 8

THE SYRUPY SWEET LIQUID SPLASHED coolly at the back of Chance's throat and then drained down behind his ribs. That is where the Thunderbird changed its personality, bursting into flame, searing the inside of his bird-like chest before settling into a molten churning pool in the pit of his empty stomach.

The thin boy's guts flipped and his eyes watered and for a terrifying few seconds, he even thought that he might gag, but he got himself together enough to wheeze out the words "Damn, that's some good shit."

As the wine worked its magic, thoughts of Marvelous Harriston flooded him. He wished that he had had wine to give her. If he had, this magic of the elixir he would have copped more than a feel when they had played alone behind her house.

Chance tried to conjure up images of Marvelous' large, soft breasts, but he kept getting snapshots of his grandfather. He saw the sandy road that snaked in front of Partners house. He got images of Marvelous' brothers. An array of memories from Tallahassee flooded his thoughts.

It had been two years since he made his stand not to go to Florida. He still didn't understand why his father hadn't forced him to go. Truth be told, he wished that he was there now. Not only because of Marvelous and the way she had made him feel behind her house on that summer day long ago, but because of how the Harriston kids made him feel. To them he was cool simply because he came from Cleveland. He never felt that he had to prove anything to them to garner their respect and even their awe. But with his boys, X, Biggie, Roach, and OD., he felt he was in a constant battle to gain respect, to be seen as cool.

"Man, you going give up the wine or what, punk?" Biggie spat the question as he looked disdainfully at Chance.

"Punk, give up the bottle if you don't know how to drink," Biggie barked snatching the paper-bagged wrapped wine bottle from Chance.

"Let a man show you boys how it's done." Tilting the twisted paper bag up toward the street lamp burning directly above the group of four boys, Biggie sucked down the wine.

Bathed in the stark glow of the street light Biggie's thin angular yellow face shimmered under a pile of conked sandy hair. He seemed to radiate a heat that threatened to send the orange freckles liberally sprinkling his cheeks and nose popping like kernels of corn from his smooth face.

A walnut-sized lump jumped up and down in the open collar of Biggie's purple high boy shirt, as he took a long swig from the bottle.

Belching, he dragged a hand, that was mostly spindly fingers, across his pursed lips.

"Now, that's the way a man drinks," bellowed Biggie burping again. "You hear me? A man," he yelled again up into the slate gray sky, spreading wide his gangly arms which made him look like some large yellow bird ready to take flight.

Biggie saw himself as an exotic bird of prey, a mighty winged predator, skilled at swooping down on unwary and unsuspecting young ladies, snatching them up on the talons of his sweet talk. In his mind Biggie was a lover supreme.

"They calls me sweet peter jeter a shonuff womb beater," Biggie crowed up into the night, again tilting up the paper bag, dribbling a bit of the wine on his chin, before finding his lips.

Biggie's mother, Ula Jean Butler, also saw her youngest child, Julian Turner Butler, with wings, but those belonging to a perfect angel. Of course Biggie's mother viewed anything that was an extension of her, as perfection, and she couldn't be dissuaded otherwise, no matter the evidence to the contrary.

But to be fair, Biggie was a very different person around his mother, who as owner of one of the largest black-owned real estate companies in Cleveland, Butler and Butler Incorporated, was a well-ensconced member of the Negro elite. Biggie's mom was keenly aware of her social status, which she had worked so diligently to achieve in an effort to overcome her less than distinguished Alabama roots.

She thought she had attained that goal when she married Biggie's father, William Turner Butler, not long after her returned from World War II, having served in Italy driving supply trucks as part of the famed Red Ball Express.

The Cleveland Call & Post, which weekly told the stories of the comings and goings in the black community that were ignored by Cleveland's two daily papers, ran a two-page spread of the wedding, the social event of 1947. While the story barely mentioned Ula Jean, or her husband William for that matter, it went on extensively about the Butler family, which was for all intents and purposes was its patriarch, Julian Butler. It was the senior Butler, who in 1925 with "only a used horse drawn wagon built a Negro business empire" trumpeted the article. It was an empire that included a moving company, several apartment buildings and a recently established real estate firm that was to be run by his son, a World War II hero, Biggie's dad, William.

Much to her disappointment Ula Jean's marriage into the Butler family and its many social and civic club affiliations hadn't immediately yielded the social benefits she was sure would come with the affixing of the Butler name to hers. For the most part she was snubbed by the high-tone Negro society, slights that didn't upset her as much as did her husband's nonchalant attitude toward the situation. His "what does it matter, baby, they're just a bunch of stuff shirts" response to the social snubs only made her more determined to be a stuff shirt.

It took her awhile, years of currying favor and sucking up to women, who for the most part found it impossible to recall her name. But she finally achieved her mantle of social acceptance, which she jealously guarded, always aware of maintaining a certain image of sophistication and culture, which she made sure was ingrained in her children.

If he could, Biggie would have loved to shed most of his social status, particularly being a Jack and Jill club member. The group, which was for the children of well-placed Negroes, who were handpicked for the honor, just didn't fit Biggie's image of himself. Jack and Jill was square.

Maybe, if any of his friends had been members it wouldn't have been so bad – the teas, the formal dances and all. But membership would have never been extended to any of his friends because their parents weren't in the right social circles.

And although Biggie never talked about it, there was no denying that his mother was a big woman in the Negro community and not only because she stood 6' 1". She was one of the realtors who opened up the Lee Harvard community to blacks. As working class blacks and newly minted middle-class blacks moved up from and away from Mt. Pleasant and the Fairfax neighborhoods, with its small, but sturdy older frame homes and two-family houses, she steered them into the larger solid brick abodes that had belonged mainly to elderly whites living in Lee Harvard.

Because of her home selling skill, Mrs. Butler made the white newspapers in the summer of 1963. However, instead of being featured glowingly, she was derided in several editorials for employing a blockbusting strategy that was undercutting the Lee Harvard neighborhood, spurring panic selling by white residents in the face of a "Negro flood" sweeping over the area.

While the whites rushed to get out, they didn't do anything as foolhardy as selling their homes at distressed prices. If anything the whites made a killing selling to blacks, greatly inflating the price of their homes. Mrs. Butler also made out well representing not only many of the Negro buyers but more than a few white sellers as well.

Besides his membership in Jack and Jill, which required him to attend a formal cotillion every other year, the other source of shame in Biggie's life, although he would deny it, was his father, the silent Butler of Butler and Butler.

Standing maybe 5' 5" on his toes, his father figuratively and literally lived in the shadow of his wife. She was the boss and he was the employee. However, the arrangement had never bothered Mr. Butler, because he wasn't a driven businessman and was content handling the office paperwork. It made perfect sense to him to let his gregarious, hard-driving wife do what she did best, go out, meet people and grow the business. She enjoyed small talk and hobnobbing but not as much as driving a hard bargain. He, on the other hand, was shy and preferred putting in a few hours at the office and then going home to plop down in front of the television set. He didn't need black tie award dinners, or civic proclamations, he didn't need the spotlight, or seats on various Negro business boards. He didn't like going to war on the battlefield of business. He was a conscientious objector when it came to squeezing someone with an iron clad contract.

Yes, Mr. Butler was happy with the arrangement with Mrs. Butler, even if his son wasn't.

After years of hoping that his father would stand up to his mother, instead of just sitting passively as she ranted about some administrative problem he wasn't handling in the way she would have handle it. Or her questioning him at the top of her lungs, why he wasn't more help, and why everything was always on her — Biggie changed allegiance. He had eventually gotten to the point where he enjoyed seeing his father berated by his mother. His father was a hen-pecked punk, who got exactly what he deserved, Biggie thought.

What Biggie thought he deserved was to be the cock of the walk. Of course, Biggie was no fool and he was mindful not to crow around his mama, and especially not like he crowed in the streets.

"Hey, man save me a corner," demanded O. D., afraid that Biggie was going to drain the wine bottle.

"Fuck you. I bought the Gawd damn wine!" Biggie spat back, trying to shove O. D. away. But O. D. wasn't about to be moved. He thrust out a half a ham hand.

"Man, just hand over the bottle," said O. D. again matter of factly, his hand outstretched, palm upward and not a hint of menace in his whispered voice.

"I don't have to do nothing. I bought the damn wine. Hell, y'all drank up the other bottle. It's only right that the man who bought the shit finish it off," barked Biggie, peering over the top of his black-rimmed, green-tinted, prescription shades.

"Man, you ain't bought shit. You stole it, just like you stole that jacked-up outfit off Bozo the damn Clown," X, snorted, easing up next to O. D. as the alley exploded with laughter.

"Fuck y'all," snapped Biggie, quickly turning up the bag and sucking down the last of the wine in four loud gulps.

"Here O. D. you want the corner?" Biggie turned the bottle upside down to show that it was empty and then threw it on the ground between them. The bag muffled the sound of smashing glass.

"There's your damn corner, big man," cackled Biggie, wiping the corners of his mouth, pulling down at his lips with a thumb and index finger.

"Biggie, why you got to do some messed up stuff like that?" asked Chance.

"Cus the boy's a punk," said X as he stepped up into Biggie's chest, his hands balled in fists at his sides.

When it came to scrapping, X wasn't shy. He didn't let the fact that he was only 5'6", 125 pounds sopping wet, stop him from getting up into anyone's face. X was ready to throw down in a heartbeat.

"Forget it, man. Biggie's just fucked up," said O. D., flicking sparkles of glass from his pant legs with a beefy finger, his calm deep voice defusing the situation. "Let' s just get to steppin' and connect with Roach," he continued. O. D. placed a catcher mitt hand on X's scrawny shoulder and pulled him out of Biggie's chest.

O. D. never got angry, at least none of his friends had ever seen him really mad nor heard him speak in any tone much above a whisper. God knew what he was doing giving O. D. an even temper and a passive nature, particularly since O. D. had always been big.

In the sixth grade he was 5'-10 and a solid 140 pounds. By the time he was 13, O. D. had packed on another 60 pounds and stretched up to 6 feet, and at 16, 220 and 6' 2", O. D. was still growing. That is why the football coaches had drooled when they caught a glimpse of O. D. at 10th grade orientation for the John F. Kennedy class of 1970, just a few months earlier.

Although he was just a sophomore and had never played anything more organized than pick-up touch football games in the street, Coach Reed had already mentally penciled in O. D.'s name on the varsity rooster. When Coach Reed finally convinced him to try out for the team, his visions of an East Senate Cleveland school district championship faded, but grudgingly.

"You got to be mean if you want to play this game, son. Junk yard dog mean." That was the constant refrain of the exasperated coaching staff for four frustrating weeks. That's how long it took to finally dash their hopes.

Mean just wasn't in O. D. When Coach Reed came to understand that he let O. D. turn in his helmet and pads and the coach let go of his dreams of what might have been.

Yet, O. D., despite his nature, had an unwarranted reputation for being menacing, which had marked him as a troublemaker almost since entering school. Because of his size most of the teachers at Gracemount Elementary, most of the women and whites, were afraid of O. D. and tried their best to avoid him. It didn't matter to them that his last name started with a D, Osceola Davis, was always placed at the back of the class as far away from the teacher's desk as possible.

When he got to Charles W. Elliot Junior High, the white male teachers thought that they needed to establish who the boss was and would get in O. D.'s face for the smallest infraction. Nor did it help matters that O. D. was also hard of hearing, which caused him to respond slowly when spoken to. That, coupled with being perpetually seated at the back of the classroom just made a bad situation worse.

O. D.'s tardy response to a teacher's question, or command, caused him to be labeled insolent, a troublemaker with a chip on his shoulder, a big colored kid, who bore watching.

O. D. was aware of how many of his teachers thought of him and he realized he was treated differently, even unfairly because of his size, and what the teachers thought was an attitude problem. Yet, he never let it bother him too much, not even when he was held back in the sixth grade because of a "surly attitude."

Mrs. Werner, O. D.'s sixth grade teacher, refused to assist him when she saw he was falling behind in his work. When O. D. got around to working up the nerve to ask why she refused to call on him when he raised his hand with a question, Mrs. Werner became indignant and sent him to the office. From that day on, she had made it up in her mind that she was going to break O. D. That year she had him suspended four times. Mrs. Werner wanted the "big insolent bully" out of her class and she was determined to let him know she wasn't going to tolerate a "brute."

Like their eldest son, O. D.'s parents were passive and didn't like making waves so they never challenged Ms. Werner, or questioned her decision to flunk their son.

O. D. had come by his subdued, non-aggressive, easy going style naturally. That is why Chance, but even more so X, took offense to Biggie bullying O. D. Biggie knew that O. D. wouldn't rear up on his haunches no matter how much you yanked his chain, so he relentlessly picked at him, teased him, and sometimes humiliated him.

It was Chance's dream that O. D. would one day just haul off and tag Biggie upside his yellow, processed head, with one of those mallets O. D. passed off as fists. Chance was wishing that his dream would come true at that very moment, but the moment quickly passed.

"I ain't studin' Big," drawled O. D., wrapping an arm around X's shoulder leading him out the alley.

"We gots to get to steppin' if we gointa hook up with Roach," insisted O. D., this time catching Chance with his other arm and dragging his two friends along up the street.

"Shit, the mothafuckin three fag-a-teers," shouted Biggie at their backs.

"Your mama," spat X, a hint of danger tingeing his retort.

Biggie, picking up on the menacing tone, decided not to get into a game of the dozens with X, figuring correctly that X was just looking for a reason to throw down on him.

"Yeah, let's get with O. D. and Roach 'fore them fools eat up all the good shit," Biggie, said breaking out in a jog.

On Saturdays, Roach, the nickname that Lindsey Harris couldn't stand, but couldn't shed despite numerous fist fights and at least one brick-throwing incident, got off work as a bus boy at Art's at 5:30 p. m.

As a rule he came in early on Saturdays, just after 6 a. m., catching the combination early morning and late night crowd. The charred, black grill sizzled with steaks, strips of bacon and buckwheat flap jacks, while pots of grits and Art's Red Rooster's famous bouillabaisse bubbled above the stoves blue-yellow flame.

Art's never closed. It was a 24-7 operation, with a loyal clientele that ranged from pimps and hoes to big-time preachers and doctors and everyone else in between.

Clocking out at the height of the dinner hour meant things were hectic in Art's kitchen, which meant Roach could swipe a steak or two, a half a chicken, and even an occasional lobster tail without being noticed, that is if he was careful.

This evening, because a convention of Negro accountants was in town and probably half of the conferees were in the restaurant, the kitchen was bedlam. No one noticed when Roach stuffed two tin foil wrapped bundles inside an empty lard can, which he had sat on top of a box of trash he hauled outside. Inside the tin can, balled in foil were a thick porterhouse steak, two broiled chicken breasts, and an order of fried shrimp scampi.

When Chance and the rest finally reached the rendezvous point with Roach, at a battered CTS bus shelter, a half block from Art's Red Rooster, only one chicken breast was left.

Sitting in the bus stop, two empty bottles of RC cola leaning up against the back of the corrugated metal shelter, Roach chewed contently, dipping his hand in and out of a large bag of potato chips drenched with a half bottle of Red Devil hot sauce.

The shelter exploded around Roach as Chance, X, and O. D. marked their arrival at the preappointed spot by banging their fists rapid fire at the back of the shelter. The percussive greeting startled Roach so, that he dropped his half-empty bag of chips, which spread across the concrete at his feet.

"Damn, why y'all always got to be screwing round," whined Roach, snatching up the potato chip bag accessing his loss.

"What's up my Ace Boon Coon?" chirped Biggie as he rounded the side of the shelter and plopped down on its wooden bench, its surface covered with hearts and initials gouged into the splintered wood.

O. D. and X immediately reached for the tin foil package sitting between Biggie and Roach on the wooden bench.

"Damn, you greedy," announced X, as he fingered back the foil to reveal the remains of the steak and the discarded tails of a dozen shrimp.

"Ain't nobody told y'all to be so slow," said Roach, pulling a chicken bone from between his greasy lips. "I tried to save you'll some but I was hungry."

"What's that behind your back?" O. D. lunged at Roach and snatched the tin foil package pressed between Roach and the corner of the shelter. O. D. stiff armed Roach to the side, scooped up the ball of silver and dashed out of the shelter. He looked like Jim Brown exploding through a defensive line. Chance and X bounced off O. D. like a pair of over-matched hapless tacklers, O. D. charging down the street, his tin foil football of food cradled tight to his body.

For a fat kid O. D. was fast and he quickly outdistanced X and Chance, who only half-heartedly gave chase. Once he knew he and his prize were safe, O. D. opened the crumpled foil, and pulled out a crispy, brown fried chicken breast and bite off a huge chunk.

He had so much chicken stuffed into his mouth that he almost gagged trying to chew.

"Ya don know wha ya miffin," O. D. mumbled through the mash of chicken wadded in his mouth as he worked his jaws mightily.

"I don't believe you," Chance said shaking his head as he turned to Roach.

"Didn't save your boys even a few crumbs."

"Hell, I see you didn't save me any wine," observed Roach, as he balled up the remains of his repast in foil and arched a jump shot into trash barrel next to the shelter.

"Yeah, where's the wine?" asked O. D. as he waddled back to the group, lifting his leg to cut loose a long, loud fart.

"Damn, you a nasty nigga," spat Biggie, which proved even more offensive to the group than the fart.

Nigger was the one word that none of them used. It wasn't like the other cuss words, it carried a special significance all its own. It was a word that if a grown-up heard would get the taste slapped out of a kid's mouth.

When he was younger, maybe 6 or 7, Chance remembered raising the red ire of his father when he was reciting the ditty that all kids knew-Inney, Meany, Minny, Moe. His father was driving at the time and he immediately twisted the car over to the curve, shot around in his seat, his face blood red and his loud breath hot on Chance's, wide-eyed face.

"Don't let me ever hear you say that again. Do you understand me, boy?" His voice growing louder with every syllable.

Chance didn't understand and his questioning eyes watered in fear and confusion. His father didn't seem to hear his wife's protest that Chance didn't know what he was getting angry about.

"The kids say tiger. Catch a tiger by the toe," she tried to explain, clutching her son close to her.

"I don't give a good Gawdamn. I don't want to hear it again. Do you understand me, boy? Look at me when I'm talking to you. Do you understand me?"

Chance remembered nodding yes and then crumbling into his mother's bosom.

"Don't call me that again," growled O. D.

"Yeah, and I'm going to break me off a piece of your yellow ass, too," X chimed in.

Biggie opened his mouth to respond but decided the best thing to do was just to let the touchy issue die.

Roach stepped out into the silence. "So what's the plan? We going to that party up in Shaker later tonight or what?" Before he could get the question out of his mouth good, a black and white police cruiser slowed, then stopped in front of the shelter. The boys watched the two white policeman inside, who nodded conspiratorially at one another. They eyed Chance and his friends for another long second or two and then drove away.

Chance felt a tightening in his jaw and he glanced over at X to gauge the reaction of his volatile friend, but there was no reading the vacant stare in X's eyes.

There was a long silence that was finally broken when O. D. made a loud sucking noise on the chicken bone he twirled in his lips.

"Let's hat before they decide to come back," said O. D.

When Chance turned to acknowledge the tug at his sleeve, his eyes slammed into Roach who simply nodded and began walking slowly from the shelter. O. D. and Biggie followed suit.

Finally, X snapped on his heels, slide a hand into the waistband of his pants and broke down a little to the right. Dipping the shoulder of his free hand so it could swing loosely at his side, he sauntered away in an arrogant, stiff-leg pimp as he tailed his friends up the street.

The cop car did a U-turn, slowed and kept pace with them for eight or nine seconds before speeding off down the road.

"Muthafuckers, mutha fucker, mutha fucker," Roach shouted, landing two vicious uppercuts into the air.

"When Stokes becomes mayor he's gonna get rid of crackers like that." Roach pointed at the cop car fading in the distance and then shouted. "Things gonna change when Stokes runnin' this city!"

"They just pissed cus they know they going to be taking orders from a Negro soon, that's all." The pronouncement immediately lifted Chance's spirits.

"Don't go counting your chickens before they hatch. He still got to win the election and that's a couple months away," warned Biggie, although he had already overheard his mother on the phone speculating, who among her friends and business associates would be filling what positions in Carl Stokes' administration.

"Them cracker cops know what's coming, that's why they fucked with us. They can't stand the fact that we going to be running this here city," said X, stretching out his hand to slap five to Chance as he turned to

Biggie. "Give me one of them squares."

Biggie shook two Kool cigarettes from the green cellophane pack and passed one to X. The other he tapped on the back of his hand before slipping it into the corner of his mouth.

Touching a match to the cigarette, Biggie drew in deeply, letting the menthol smoke drift through his body before snorting it out his nose.

"Yeah, things are going to change and these honkies best to get ready," Biggie said hoarsely as he coughed up a small cloud.

The boys again walked in silence.

"So, what about tonight? Where we goin?" asked Biggie, stopping to light-up another cigarette.

"Yeah, what's the happs?" Roach piped in.

"Man, what you talkin'' bout? Boy, look at you."

"What?" A look of genuine pain of Roach's face.

"I know you going home to change. Look at you looking like Patches," cracked Chance.

"Patches, we depending on your son," sang X, Biggie, Chance and O. D. in unison.

"I got my shit right here in the bag," said Roach, holding up a crumpled A&P grocery bag. "Just stop off at a gas station restroom, splash on a little water. Dab on a little smell good and I will be ready for Freddy."

"Oh, hell naw. You'll chase away all the babes. You better get home and scrub your rusty ass," Biggie cracked, which touched off an eruption of laughter.

"Fuck y'all" was all Roach could muster in the way of defense.

Roach wasn't about to risk going home to change. He knew there would be a good chance that his parents, if they weren't passed out drunk, would make him stay home and watch his three brothers and two sisters.

From past experience the boys also knew that waiting on Roach to extricate himself from his house once he stepped through the door was at best a very dicey situation. Sometimes Roach could rush in, grab what he needed and holler his goodbyes over a shoulder as he charged out the door. However, more often than not Roach would be waylaid by his mother, who would then lay a few chores on him or plead for help watching the kids, which often included several cousins. There were so many kids in and out of the Harris house that some folks had taken up saying that the Harrises multiplied like roaches. At some point the name had attached to Lindsey.

"I ain't going nowhere near my crib tonight. I got a Bly knit in a bag and a half-bottle of High Karate and I bet a pull more broads than any of you fools with your tired raps."

"Well, take your High Karate ass over to that Sohio and make this transformation," said Chance pointing to the gas station half way up the block. "We'll wait for you up at Whitmores, so the rest of us can get something to eat since you dicked us on the grub."

"Man, order me a Polish boy while you up there," said Roach digging in his pockets and extracting a wadded dollar bill and some change.

"I don't believe you. You mean you still hungry? Your ass should weigh 300 pounds the way you be eating." X's mouth dropped at the prospect of Roach eating anymore food.

Roach rolled his eyes up in his head and pressed the money into Chance's hand.

"Damn, I don't need all this crap. Chance, just get me a Polish boy alright?" With that, Roach dodged the traffic clogging Lee Road and jogged toward the Sohio station.

The heavy smell of charcoal and burning wood, a mixture of hickory and oak, basted in the dripping fat from slabs of pork, filled the small narrow room. The room was made even tighter by the two pop machines and juke box that lined the right wall and the line of six orange plastic chairs that bumped up against each other on the left wall. The furnishings created a three-foot wide aisle way that ran the ten feet from the front door of Whitemore's Bar-B-Que to the four-foot- high, blue Formica-topped counter that was lined with Saran-wrapped desserts.

A young woman standing behind the counter leaned over and rested an elbow near a wedge of coconut cream pie. Beads of sweat glistened on her mahogany brown, unlined forehead. She looked up from under penciled-in eyebrows and between smacks of gum asked, "This going to be one check?"

"Naw, I'm payin' for my order. Them clowns are on their own." O. D. threw a thumb over his shoulder at Chance, Biggie and X, who had crowded in behind him.

"Give me a shoulder dinner and put extra sauce on the fires," said O.D. gazing up at the sign above the counter. White numbers and letters, many of them missing, were spaced along rows of red ridges and spelled out Whitmore's bill of fare.

Shrt Ribs $3.-5, Slab $7.25, Polsh bOy $2, Shlder Diner $3.5o...

"Hold it. Change that to a short rib dinner and let me have an extra slice of bread with that." O.D. licked his lips, still not sure of his orders.

"You still want extra sauce with that, honey?" She rolled her eyes as she scratched on a green order pad that she cupped in her hand.

O.D. nodded.

She ripped a page from the pad and slapped it onto the ledge of the window-like opening behind her. Turning she said "next" in a flat, bored voice that match the look on her pudgy face.

Chance wedged next to O.D., his back turned to the woman at the counter as he, X and Biggie debated their order.

"Anytime will do, honey," sighed the woman sucking her large yellow teeth as she shifted her bulk from her left leg to her right, a stubby, gnawed blue pencil at the ready.

"Okay, how much for two dozen fried chicken wings with sauce?" asked Chance as he turned to the woman.

"*Thweet.*" She sucked her teeth again. "Well, let's see here," she said mockingly as she turned, leaned back against the counter, its edge sinking deep into her fleshy hips. "It says wings are ten cents each and you want two dozen. That's still 24, isn't it?"

Getting the point, Chance continued. "Yeah, two dozen wings and a half pound of fries with sauce."

The woman held her pencil to the pad but didn't write. Instead she stared at Chance one eyebrow arched.

"You sure now? Cause I got better things to do than to be writing and erasing." She shot a look at O.D. When Chance didn't reply, she scribbled on her pad, ripped another green rectangle from her order pad and turned to the opening behind her, this time a hand reached out and accepted the paper.

"Sauce on the fries, Sally?" asked the hand.

Sally peeked over her shoulder and lifted an eyebrow.

"Yes, please. Sauce on the fries," stammered Chance, who had just remembered he had forgotten to order a Polish boy for Roach.

"That's another fifty cents. *Thweet.*"

The attitude that was clear in the sound of Sally sucking her teeth dissuaded Chance from adding a Polish boy to his order. Roach would just have to face Sally himself.

They were standing in the eight car parking lot, which served Whitmore's, Monique's House of Style beauty shop and Colson's Sundries, dipping hands in and out of two grease-stained boxes, when Roach approached. His cologne reached Chance and the others a good 10 seconds before Roach did.

"Where's my sandwich?"

Wiping his hands in two napkins, Chance retrieved $1.85 from his pocket and reached it out to Roach.

"What's this?"

"You can go in and order it yourself. I didn't want it to get cold," said Chance, pulling another wing from the box, sucking sauce from his fingers.

Roach looked at the line, which was almost out the door, leading to the counter and slipped the money back into his pocket. "Let me grab a wing."

"Okay, so where we headin' ?" asked Roach between bites.

The question caught the rest of the group cold. They hadn't really finalized their plans. Usually there were several house parties being held on Friday and Saturday nights, the invitations passed out during study hall on small slips of paper.

Tonight the pickings were slim. There was a waistline party, where they looped a tape measure around your mid-section to determine your admission. According to the dog-eared square of paper in Biggie's palm, it was being held from 9 until (until somebody's daddy flicked on the basement lights and personally ushered everyone out the door) on Dove Avenue.

X had been told by a cousin about another party in Shaker Heights, but he couldn't remember the address.

"I think he said it was on Abbington or Abbingdale or something like that," said X.

"That's too far to be going on a maybe," complained Chance, who was more than a bit upset with X. If he had a definite address it would be no question that the Shaker party would have been the destination because the girls who went to Shaker were "some kind of fine."

"Damn, X, why didn't you get it straight when you talked to him?" moaned

Chance, the thought of missing out on some high-yellow, good hair Shaker Heights girl gnawing at him.

"Don't blame me. It was my cousin who wasn't sure."

"Ahha," groaned Biggie dismissing X with a disgusted wave.

"Well, I ain't about to go down on Dove Avenue. That's down in Wee Delamore territory and I don't feel like getting into no fight tonight." Roach was referring to the gang who claimed the streets around John Adams as their turf. He didn't get any argument from the others.

"Well, it looks like the only option we got left is this one." Chance unfolded the slip of paper and held it out for the rest to see.

"Well, it's at least in the neighborhood," sighed O.D.

"Hell, that wouldn't have been no issue if you had gotten your old man's car like you said were." Biggie glared over at O.D.

"I didn't see you asking your mama if you could use her car," shot O.D. back and then quickly turned on Chance, Roach and X.

"And, you three underage, no driver-license, CTS bus-riding-clowns don't say a thing."

Chance threw up both his hands in mock surrender.

"So I guess we better gets to steppin then," said Chance.

"Head'em up and move-em out," shouted X.

CHAPTER 9

15610 KINGSFORD, SHAKE A TAIL FEATHER PARTY, Friday, from 8 until. 25 cents

Chance checked the numbers on the front door of the white clapboard house against the crinkled square of paper between his fingers.

"This is it," said Chance as he strode back to the top of the driveway to rejoin his knot of friends.

"You sure, man? It look kinda dead to me."

"Hell, I can read. But if you don't want to take my word for it, you trot your ass on up on the porch and check the address for yourself," Chance said extending the wrinkled slip of paper toward Biggie.

Just then the Bar Kays whispered... "Soul finger. Soul finger." The horn-driven melody wafted out from around the foundation of the house, rustled the lush green carpet of pachysandra that covered the narrow patch of ground at the side of the house, and drifted up the long asphalt drive.

"Alright," smiled X, bobbing his head and snapping his thin fingers.

"Man it still sound dead to me," huffed Biggie dismissing X with a wave. "Why don't one of y'all go check out the party and come back and let the rest of us know how it is."

Without hesitating Chance turned and started up the drive with X on his heels.

"Come back and let us know how it is," Biggie yelled at their backs.

When X and Chance got within two feet of the screened side door, it suddenly rattled open on squeaky hinges. A shaft of white light poured out at their feet and the Bar Kays' whisper turned into a roar as the music pushed its way out of torn section of wire mesh hanging limp over the bottom edge of the door.

"What it be like in there?" asked X as he reached out to steady the skinny girl who stumbled into the square of light.

"Oh, ah, thanks," she stammered startled and embarrassed. Steadying herself with a hand on X's shoulder she regained her composure.

"I got my heel caught," explained the girl lifting up a shapely white nyloned leg and reaching down to push a white high heel shoe back onto her foot.

"It's packed down there. I'll tell you what they say is true, Negroes shonuff draw some heat," she continued, pushing back her slick black bangs and dabbing a napkin at her forehead.

When she flashed her 100-watt grin on X, he flashed one equally bright right back at her. Chance took all the high-voltage cheesing as his cue to leave and he stepped up into the doorway.

"That be a quart-ta, my man," said the grinning black Buddha filling the small space of the back stairs landing. The big boy oozed over the sides of a metal stool, tufts of yellow foam rubber stuffing peeked out from gouges in the green vinyl cushion that strained under his bulk.

The Buddha's close-cropped black hair, slicked to his round dome, melted into his wide sweat glazed ebony face. The bulk jerked his high-gloss head back toward the large mason jar that sat at the top of the three steps directly behind his stool.

Chance fished two fingers into the slit pocket at the front of his lime green Continental-style sharkskin pants and with no little effort jimmied out a quarter. Leaning, he reached out and plunked the quarter onto the silvery mound of coins filling a third of the old jelly jar.

"Yo, slick, you got him covered, too?" asked black Buddha, which he did as much with his mouth as he did with the arch of his eyebrows.

Chance glanced over his shoulder in the direction pointed out by the eyebrows where X smiled sheepishly his hand at the elbow of the 100-watt girl who he guided past Buddha, past Chance and down the darkened stairwell.

Wedging the same two fingers into the slit pant pocket, Chance slid out a second quarter and dropped it into the mason jar. Before he could pull his hand back from over the rim of the jar Buddha had grabbed his wrist. The beefy paw enveloped the entire lower third of Chance's arm and held him motionless for the split second it took Buddha to slash a thick red Magic Marker check across the back of Chance's hand.

"Tell your boy he got to get his hand marked. If he leaves out and ain't got no mark, he gonnta havta drop another quarter to gets back in," rumbled the bulk, releasing the fleshy vise.

Chance instinctively rubbed at his wrist and he inspected the red mark as the feeling slowly returned to his fingers. He nodded that he understood. Buddha flexed his eyebrows and dismissed him.

Chance smoothed the front of his pants, and patted at his head, hoping that any unruly strands of hair would find their assigned place in the Dixie Peach-oiled rows of waves that rose from the part at the right side of his head and cascaded over his left ear. With a wide grin he started down the stairs.

An intoxicating mixture of soul music, high-pitched laughter and the husky whispers of small talk filtered up the shrouded stairwell. Chance hunched his shoulders and pressed his hairless chin to his chest. Half of his face disappeared in the stiff collar of his canary yellow high-boy shirt as he ducked, not wanting to bang his head on the low hanging ceiling.

Groping blindly along the sidewalls, he felt ahead cautiously with his right foot as he descended sideways into the ghoulish purple fog that hung at the bottom of the stairs. Chance stumbled off the last step, which was tilted badly to one side, but quickly recovered his balance.

His eyes watered as they tried to adjust to the darkness, which was only the slightest bit disturbed by the single blue-light bulb stuffed in the ceiling. Chance squinted out on the scene before him. Bumping and twisting silhouettes gyrated in choppy motions in the center of the cramped basement.

A long, leaning line of prescription-shade wearing, dick-holding, too cool dudes, their broad, flat arrogant noses, illuminated by cigarettes that limply clung to fleshy bottom lips, held up the basement's white cinderblock walls.

A black plastic tower of 45s, which stood erect in the center of a boxy hi-fi, clicked down another of its monaural number. The basement vibrated with the warble of saxophone-backed, falsetto harmony ..."the way you stole my heart, whowho, you could have been a cool crook and baby you so smart, whowho, you could have been a school book..."

A lone window at the far side of the basement, pushed out on its hinges, greedily sucked at the dark, smoke-streaked fog.

A hint of a smile eased into the corners of Chance's mouth as he realized that he had indeed invested his quarter well.

"Alright," chimed in X smiling and slapping five with Chance.

The wine-glazed floor grudgingly released its adhesive grip on the soles of their shoes as they waded into the hot, sweat-sweet sea of dancing bodies. Guided by smoldering orange cigarette beacons, they inched across the basement.

Chance and X, their heads cocked haughtily back, each with a hand pensively stroking a hairless chin, lips pursed, jaws taut, they copped a mean lean and fell into the line against the cinderblock wall and proceeded to check out "da ladies."

Barely embracing, floating in a safe space of arms that encircle but don't really touch, Chance and Mavis danced.

His arms hung timidly around her tiny waist, not daring to rest on the fullness of her hips.

Her arms were around his neck, but consciously resisted the warm support of his shoulders.

Mavis and Chance, two people shadow dancing, keeping a safe space of anonymity between them. Two people not daring to breath too deeply, not daring to speak. Both of them frightened of the rejection any familiarity, no matter how innocent, or polite, could bring.

"Why did I ask her to dance?" Chance thought to himself as nervousness closed tighter around him.

She wasn't even his type. She was not the fine sort of heifer that his boys would slap him five for, envious that they hadn't been the one to grind against her.

No, she wasn't that type of fine that jumps out at you from a blaze of yellow skin and a flood of good hair.

But Chance knew full well what he had gotten himself into. He had stolen quick glances of Mavis all night.

For most of the evening Mavis had sat unnoticed, at least that is what she had thought, on the red vinyl couch where she danced to every record without once leaving her seat. That had suited her just fine, since nearly all of her dancing was limited to her bedroom in front of a dresser mirror where any risk of embarrassment was unlikely, unless her little sister or brother barged into her room.

Mavis probably would have passed the entire evening away, bouncing and swaying on the couch if her cousin Bernadette hadn't nearly snatched her arms out of their sockets to get her to dance the "Cool Jerk."

"Girl, you know that's your song. Get on up here and dance," said Bernadette, refusing to let Mavis pull away from her and retreat back to the safety of the couch.

"If I gotta dance with you, I will. But you ain't sittin' this one out. Now, get it girl."

Bernadette threw all 4 foot 10 of herself into the song. Her arms chopping up and down like pale pistons and her long auburn ponytail whipping the air.

Mavis, much less animated than her popular cousin, looked about the room to see who was watching them. Sure that they weren't being singled out from the mass of jerking bodies, Mavis threw back her head, closed her eyes and ran with the music, secure in the thought that no one was paying any mind.

Mavis hadn't seen Chance.

As he fixed on the undulating green skirt that rode high on top of a pair of black windowpane stockings, Chance wished he had downed more of that Thunderbird that he and his boys had passed among themselves as they walked to the party. If he had, he wouldn't have let Mavis dance with her cousin.

"Yo, Chance, it's comin' up after this next platter, man," said Biggie, shoving a bony elbow into Chance's side.

"Whatcha talking about?"

"Coochie crawl. Bump n' Grind. Slow drag...The Dells, Stay in my corner, my brother. The jams bout to drop and you besta be on it."

A shit-eating grin spread like spilled milk across Biggie's yellow face. Rolling his red-rimmed eyes back up into his bean head, Biggie placed his hand flat against his belly and ground his pelvis against the thick, moist air. He was no longer mad that Chance and X had left him, O.D. and Roach hanging in the drive, having failed to return with a reconnaissance report on the party.

"Man, you best select you a hoe now if you plans to get in on this dry hump," said Biggie still grinning as he scanned the room for a victim.

"You gonna miss out, boy, if you don't move," added X, who was being pulled into the press of bodies by the 100-watt girl.

Chance turned and looked over at the red couch.

She wasn't there. She hadn't returned to the couch after the Cool Jerk had faded out.

The green skirt with black windowpane stockings wasn't among the hand dancers, who now commanded the floor, either.

Chance felt the first icy pricks of panic clutching him. Then he spied her fanning herself under the open basement window.

Sucking in a deep breath, Chance started toward the window. He hoped that the stone-faced look he had slipped on would not betray the thumping creeping from his chest into the dry tightness of his throat.

Pulling away the hand that stroked his hairless chin, Chance slid it slowly, palm up in Mavis' direction. He let it hang in mid-air for just a second, ready to front her off with a torrent of loud, foul-mouthed insults if she foolishly refused his invitation to dance.

Surprised that someone had actually asked her to dance Mavis moved slowly, so slow in fact that she nearly felt the sting of Chance's face-saving bluster. But she touched his hand, flashing a nervous smile that she held down close to her small chest, too shy to look into the directness of eyes.

Mavis was glad someone had asked her to dance. It was something she really hadn't expected since she knew she wasn't popular and would never be the center of attention in a room full of high yellow girls like her cousin Bernadette.

For as long as Mavis could remember she had compared herself to Bernadette and girls like her. She longed for their coffee with extra cream skin, Bernadette even lighter with jewels of freckles on her bobbed nose.

When Mavis looked in the mirror it was a broad nose and fleshy nostrils that flared across her dark brown face that stared back at her.

She had cursed the mirror for as long as she could remember.

Sometimes she tried to convince herself that her large almond eyes were beautiful and gave her an exotic look that people found mysterious and maybe even, well, attractive. But Mavis wasn't a very persuasive girl.

Most of the time she cried.

When she cried, memories she tried to keep submerged would flood to the surface.

"Lawd have mercy, Helen. You and Joe reached way back for some of dem African genes to come up with little Mavis."

Uncle Brother would double over with laughter. The last time that he made that observation he nearly dropped the jelly jar of gin and ice he held in a skinny hand, his laughter came so hard. Uncle Brother's unchallenged ability to play the dozens brought him more joy than nearly anything else on God's green earth.

"Hush you ugly mouf. Don't go talking about my baby in my house," Helen had scolded. But there was a giggle in her voice that she hoped her daughter didn't detect.

"Joe, all that black must come from your side of the family. Lord knows me and my sister Helen's ancestors didn't stand for none of that mess," said Uncle Brother, laughing so loud that it seemed to rattle the dishes in the cupboards. Uncle Brother was so tickled with himself that he sloshed gin on the front his shirt.

Mavis knew she shouldn't take it personally; Uncle Brother picked on and teased everyone. No one was spared his razor wit, and slashing tongue. No one that is except his mother, Mavis' Grandma Grace.

Grace didn't tolerate Uncle Brother's "devilish foolishness... If you ain't got nothing good to say then keep your lips zipped," she would say.

Uncle Brother didn't come around much when Grandma Grace came to Cleveland for her annual visit. She would come two days before Christmas and leave exactly four days later.

"I got's to be in my house to start the new year," explained the old lady.

Everyone in the family was glad to see Grace board the bus and head back to Nicholasville, Kentucky. To say that she was a demanding woman was not doing Grace Thomas justice. It was her way or no way and no one ever neared her standards. When she boarded the bus, slowly stepping up sideways on arthritic legs, rebuffing any assistance with a swipe of her ebony cane, the entire family exhaled feeling free to breathe again. It wouldn't surprise any of her kin if Grace found fault with the way her family members took in air.

But for Mavis, Grandma Grace could never stay long enough to suit her. When she listened to her uncles, aunts, parents, and her two sisters gripe about Grace Thomas' hanky ways she couldn't understand their complaints. Mavis had never experienced the Grace that they described.

"Will you brush your old Grandmother's hair, Baby Girl?"

Grace already knew the answer. Mavis loved to remove the two huge tortoise shell pins that anchored a great knot of silken black at the top of her grandmother's head.

Mavis pulled out the pins and the black knot unfurled in waves around her grandmother's shoulders and over the hump at the back of her neck before cascading down her back to her ample waist, a tribute to her love of rich food and Kentucky bourbon.

Mavis, kneeling on the bed behind the old woman, slid a slender bare arm under the curtain of black hair and lifted it up and away from her grandmother's back. As Mavis slowly pulled a large silver-back brush with yellow bristles through the mane of hair, Grace would retell the family history.

Mavis gloried in her family's past and marveled at all the different types of blood that coursed through her veins proud Africans, Creek and Cherokee Indian and a smattering of French and German. Grandma Grace could see all the branches of the family tree in Mavis face.

"I saw the same things in my sister Harriet's face. My sister and you, Baby Girl, could have been twins. You're your great-aunt Harriet all over. Same calm face. Same big, deep, mysterious eyes and same neon bright smile," Grandma Grace exclaimed in her high-pitched voice, punctuating the statement with a hiccup of a laugh.

"It's a smile that lights up a room. Just lights the room, Baby Girl."

That's what Grandma Grace would always say as she repinned her hair and then cupped Mavis' beaming face between her fleshy palms and planted a juicy kiss on her forehead for emphasis.

"Harriet all over again. Smile that lights the room."

Mavis was glad that the basement was dark. If it hadn't been dark she was sure that this boy holding her tight would have never asked her to dance.

No, she wasn't jump-out-at-you fine, Chance thought. Yet, there was something extremely appealing about this black girl in his arms. Something that he couldn't put into words but liked very much.

Mavis was so rich in her darkness that she seemed to glow. It was a glow that gave off an intoxicating heat that warmed Chance at that very moment.

Chance had seen her before walking the halls between classes at J. F. K High, but he hadn't really seen her, at least not like he was seeing her now during this dance, during this slow drag.

No, that wasn't true, Chance said to himself correcting his musings. He may not have noticed Mavis but he hadn't miss seeing her body. Hell, there was no way he could have missed that big round ass. He had watched mesmerized as it bounced to the Cool Jerk.

Mavis' butt was the only bold and aggressive thing about her. It refused to surrender to the painful shyness and self-doubt that stifled the rest of her being.

In truth, it was Mavis' shyness and not her butt that had really drawn Chance to her. It's why he had asked her to dance; he certainly wouldn't have risked it otherwise. Chance felt sure that someone as shy as Mavis would certainly not mention it if he lost the beat. And, she wouldn't say anything to blow his game if she somehow peeped his hold card and realized hat he was as full of self-doubt as she.

Chance sensed instinctively that she wouldn't make fun of him for his lack of worldliness.

He sensed that if he wanted to, he could drop the macho mask he wore whenever he wasn't at home, and just be himself with her.

Feeling even more at ease, he pulled her closer.

"You feel good," he heard a voice say that sounded strangely like his own.

Mavis said even more in reply by simply resting her check against his shoulder.

"Stay Darling. Stay in my corner. Ooowhoo...," the Dells crooned.

Chance and Mavis floated.

Two rapid bursts of white light flooded the basement.

"This is the last record," came an adult voice from the top of the stairs.

The bare light bulb flashed white twice more.

Chance was still holding Mavis' hand, keeping her on the dance floor.

Smokey Robinson crackled from the hi-fi, promising to build someone a castle with a tower so high until it reached the sky.

"Can I have this last dance?" asked Chance.

"I would love to dance."

With that she rested her head on his shoulder and gently searched out a comfortable position, which her hot-combed tresses immediately marked with a greasy Royal Crown smudge.

His arms, encircling her waist, pulled her closer.

Their legs entwined tightly like clinging vines.

Chance felt the softness of her breast against the front of his high-boy shirt and he flared his nostrils to take in her oven warm sweet scent.

Back and forth. Side to side, they rocked.

Chance felt more than excitement rising in him. Mavis felt it too and pressed closer against his firmness.

Chance wanted to speak. He wanted to say something smooth. At that moment, he wanted to say anything; but the words lodged in his throat. He finally gave up on saying anything at all. Instead he shut his eyes and laid his head softly against hers.

"I'm glad you asked me to dance," she said softly.

"Me too," whispered Chance, finding it a struggle to even free those few words from his mouth.

"If that won't do I'll try something new..." Chance harmonized with Smokey as he let his palms melt slowly down the smooth cool fabric of Mavis' skirt and come to rest on the roundness it covered.

A sigh echoed in Chance's ears and his dry trembling lips brushed the coarse hairs at the back of her neck.

Mavis drew in a long, deep breath, which Chance exhaled.

"I'm glad you asked me to dance," sighed Mavis again.

Chance smiled as they pressed their bodies together even harder, making small tight circles with their hips.

Mavis felt herself becoming dizzy, like she had been furiously spun around by her arms and then placed on uneasy legs and told to walk. But instead of blacking out, the sensation emboldened her.

"I hope you will walk me home," Mavis hummed as the music grew softer, then faded into silence.

"Hope you walk me home," several mocking male voices giggled.

Mavis ignored them.

Chance wanted to ignore them too. He wanted to shove the voices of his boys out of his mind, out of his life. But he couldn't.

Responding to the familiar cackles, Chance dropped his arm from Mavis and eased some space between them.

Desperately, frantically, he searched her eyes for his strength. Then he looked at his antagonizers, his boys, whispering among themselves as they leaned against the basement wall.

"Will you?" she asked again, totally oblivious to Chance's situation.

Chance stood silently for what seemed to him an eternity. He wished that the brown tile floor would open under his feet and suck him down.

He thought about what it would be like to walk with Mavis' hand in his: then Chance considered his rep. "Sure, baby, I'll walk you home. You gotta leash?"

Laughter exploded from the wall.

Gritting his teeth Chance flashed a wide grin, slapped some skin to Biggie and O.D. and prayed that he could keep the water stinging the back of his eyes from showing.

Mavis didn't even try. She ran sobbing up the basement stairs.

CHAPTER 10

THE POWDER BLUE GALAXIE PURRED AS IT MOVED slowly up the asphalt drive, its yellow parking lights barely pushing aside the darkness. The car stopped and the lights evaporated yielding to the dark pre-dawn.

Chance twisted the car keys to the left shutting off the Galaxie's engine, but not its radio, which glowed a faint green light inside the car.

The shrill chirping of crickets and the muffled electric hum from the street lamp perched on a pole next to the garage, piggy backed on the night air, which drifted cool and moist through the car's open windows.

All that remained of his Boone's Farm Apple wine high was a gentle buzz that suspended Chance in a warm spectral space between consciousness and sleep.

Screwing up the volume slightly on the car radio, mindful not to wake his family inside the silent, yellow clapboard house, Chance stepped from the car and gingerly found his feet.

In slow motion he crawled up onto the Galaxie's hood and flopped spread-eagle on his back.

The heat of the car's engine radiated through its metal skin and fanned out through his thin body. The warmth pushed the radio's music from his ears and tugged his eyelids down.

Chance woke to a crimson sky and the silky, smooth harmonies of the Delfonics "*La, la, la, la, la means, I love you...*"

Maybe it was the color of that early morning sky that caused the avalanche of thoughts to come crashing down.

Or, perhaps it was the fact that Chance knew that he would eventually have to peel himself off the Galaxie's hood and go inside.

If he went in the house now and was careful to remain very quiet, maybe, just maybe, he could slip undetected into his room. But before Chance could find comfort in that remote possibility, the red daybreak barged its way back into his thoughts.

"Red. Red. Red," Chance mouthed the words silently.

Red was the color he loved and hated.

Red was the color he longed to embrace and that he prayed to avoid.

Red was the color of his father.

Loud Red. A top of the lungs, shouting Red. That was his father. It seemed to Chance that the only time his father addressed him was in a loud Red yell.

It was—"Dummy. What are you doing?...Damnit, don't let me tell you again to stop that nonsense....Where's my belt?!"

Yeah, that was the Red that damn sky had conjured up.

Chance felt anger rising in him and he longed for another bottle of wine to dilute the feeling.

For as long as he could remember, Chance was terrified of that Red.

As a child he had run from that Red, but he was never able to out sprint him. That Red would always catch up with him, squeeze him in some tight small space, get dead in his face and suck up all his air, leaving him breathless, motionless, frozen in place until that Red would make up its mind to slowly drain from his father's face.

Chance no longer ran from that Red. Not that he still wasn't frightened of it, he had just decided that he would no long show his fear.

When that Red came for him now, Chance looked it straight in its deep scowling eyes and defiantly, steeled himself to stand his ground.

No, that wasn't quite right. Chance never defied that Red; he wasn't that crazy. Instead, he had decided to take the best that Red could dish out and not flinch, or shed a tear. He was determined not to let that Red know how deeply he hurt.

There eventually would come a time, when Chance was much older, that he would come to understand that loud, yelling, volcanic Red and the dark recess it bubbled up from. He would eventually find compassion, even forgiveness for that Red.

However, that time was not now, not on the hood of the blue Galaxie on that cool morning as he stared up into all that red sky and remembered.

As a child he had been consumed with the thought of somehow ending Red's awful reign. Often Chance would sit, balled in a dark corner where he had sought refuge, squeezing back tears behind clenched eyelids and fantasize about killing Red.

Sometimes he saw himself running up behind it, catching it unaware and shoving it down the stairs.

Sometimes Chance saw himself delivering a mad flurry of karate kicks and chops to the side of Red's head.

And then there were times where he would conjure up through prayer some mysterious unearthly power that would cause Red to simply keel over dead in its tracks.

"Damn," Chance cursed, slamming his fist hard on the car hood, feeling angry and confused.

He hated the loud, yelling Red as much as he loved that other Red.

The other Red was the red his father turned when he rocked the whole house in a convulsion of laughter. It was an out of control, watery eyed, lustful quaking of his father's soul.

A contagious laugh that grabbed hold to all who heard it and lifted them up by their hearts, dangling them wildly, joyously, into the limitless heavens before gently returning them too soon to earth.

That was the Red that wrapped Chance in invisible, strong, loving arms that made him feel warm and special. That Red wrapped him in arms that his father never extended to Chance.

That laughing Red let him in, allowed Chance to feel close to his father, to feel that he was a part of him—let him feel like his son.

But that Red was rare and came too seldom.

Both Reds came upon his father with little warning. Out of nowhere they would burst on the scene. One Red or the other would possess his father.

It was impossible for Chance to tell with any accuracy what would trigger the Reds. It seemed never to be the same thing twice. There was nothing predictable about them. That's what made the Reds so frightening and yet, so wondrous.

Like his Reds, Chance's father seemed an unfathomable mystery.

Sure, Chance was aware that his father was a well-respected pillar in the community, a man who carried weight, a man who mattered.

"Your daddy is one hell of a lawyer," some folks would say.

"He's a mover and shaker in this town. You should be proud," others would say.

Chance was proud.

Every now and then a picture of his father would appear in the local papers, not only in the Call & Post, which served Cleveland's Negro community, but also in the Press and Plain Dealer, which catered to white folks.

It always puffed Chance up when someone, particularly a teacher, would ask "Are you Eugene Marshall's son?"

The teachers who made the connection between the dark brown, colored boy in their class and the white-looking man in the newspaper photo, would read the news account aloud to the class.

Eugene Marshall, lead counsel for the Cleveland Power Corporation, commenting on a lawsuit filed against the firm said..."

Usually, it was a black teacher who made the connection.

As much as Chance enjoyed hearing the newspaper articles read in class, it was the stories about his father's childhood that he cherished most.

His father's friends, Curt, Sonny, Lloyd and Walter, dredged up the stories of their growing up black and poor in the Cleveland of the 30s and 40s, stories that provided Chance with clues about his father.

By age 10 Chance had heard the stories, in all the various versions, dozens of times.

It was Sonny who loved to tell the story of how as elementary school boys they would gorge themselves on discarded potato chips behind the old Dan Dee snack company off East 55th Street.

"Man, there was a science to eating those potato chips. You had to be careful not eat any chips from that top layer," explained Sonny, who noted that the top layers were exposed to birds, forging dogs and cats.

"Now, the trick was you had to know how far to reach down in the pile. If you dug in too deep you could end up battling rats. I lost the tip of this finger to one of the bad boys," said Sonny, who always took great pleasure in displaying his deeply nicked index finger, making sure that everyone in the room had an opportunity to view the old wound.

"Now, your daddy was the expert potato chipper. He never got bit. I'm telling you he was a natural; had a knack for finding the cleanest and freshest chips. Sometimes we would pay him to dig our chips."

It was hard for Chance to even imagine his father as a kid, let alone a kid who would scrounge for nasty potato chips.

His brothers, Lonnie and Bobby, seemed to like the potato chip story the best, but Chance's favorite was the drowning tale. All of his father's friends put their own spin on the story, and a good-hearted argument was sure to ensue as they tried to determine whose version was closer to the truth.

But no matter which of his father's friends told the story, an 8-year-old Eugene Marshall always ended up in a ditch filled with muddy water, yelling for someone to save him

When Curt told the story, he was the one who finally realized that the water was only three-feet deep and all Chance's father had to do was stand up and wade out.

Sonny and Walter also claimed to have been the one to tell Chance's father to walk out of the ditch.

However, when Lloyd told the story he actually jumped into the pool.

"It didn't matter that I couldn't swim worth a damn myself. My only thought was of saving my best friend from drowning. I think we both splashed around for several minutes, coughing, snorting, kicking and flopping around on our bellies before we realized that the water was only chest high."

Chance lived for those stories, glorious, colorful, told around the dining room table strewn with holiday remains of turkey, half-eaten macaroni casseroles, and drained bowls of chitlins and black-eyed peas.

Those boozed-up stories of fights, pranks, daring escapes and youthful romances, gave Chance snapshots of his father that he tried to match to the black and white photos that sat on the mantle; the toddler in knee pants, the boy of about 10 in an oversized coat that hung on his narrow frame like a wet wool blanket, and of the East Tech High School graduate doing his matinee idol pose.

Chance's father never spoke much during the storytelling. He simply nodded and flashed an occasional low-wattage smile, its nonchalance in stark contrast to his animated friends.

It was as if Chance's father was uneasy having so much of him being put on display and bandied about. He seemed uncomfortable with having his private memories pried into and passed around the table like a bowl of mashed potatoes, with everyone invited to plunge in and spoon up all they craved.

Chance feasted on those stories. He gorged himself, savoring every morsel, hoping to fill the emptiness he felt, hoping to satisfy his hunger for the man.

Those stories were Chance's keys to his father. Precious keys that unlocked doors his father kept bolted shut. The stories gave Chance rare opportunities to get close to his father, much closer than the almost military "Goodnight, Sir," handshakes he extended to his sons nightly as they trudged upstairs to bed.

Those stories, full of life and passion, helped to fill the suffocating silence that stood between Chance and his father. The stories allowed Chance those rare peeks behind the Red curtain that separated father from son.

Red was also the color of the strongest bond between Chance and his father - asthma.

His father's asthma was much more severe than his own. Asthma was his father's ever present nemesis, a foe that would bear hug his barrel chest several times a day, grabbing him and squeezing until it forced a saucer-eyed, "help me" red into his face and every ounce of air from his lungs.

Gasping for air, his father would clamp strained lips around a glass atomizer and with trembling fingers pump feverishly at the grey rubber bulb. Minutes passed like hours as he waited motionlessly for his lungs to clear and fill with air.

Chance longed for his infrequent bouts of wheezing, generally triggered by late spring pollen. Asthma would jump on Chance's narrow chest and double him over bug-eyed as he sucked madly for little gulps of oxygen and prayed for the understanding and tenderness his father measured out in equally small portions.

When asthma attacked Chance, his father would send a silent knowing look in his direction, a look that flooded Chance's head with words he was sure his father had wanted to say, and would have said, if he hadn't been so preoccupied with his son's physical difficulties at that moment.

Chance would feel his father's hand clasp him by the shoulders to steady him and slow his frantic breathing. With his other hand his father would pull his atomizer from his pocket and place the open end to Chance's lips.

"Take a deep breath and hold it," he would say, pumping the rubber bulb that released a fine breath giving mist of medicine.

It would take a few minutes for Chance's aching lungs to regain their composure. All the while his father stood by his side firmly patting his back.

"Better?" his father would ask.

Nodding, tears of strain flooding his eyes, Chance would smile.

"Go lay down now and take it easy," his father would say, squeezing Chance's shoulders.

Sprawling on the hood of the car, Chance remembered how he would lay in bed for hours after his asthma attacks just breathing and smiling.

His blissful reminiscence was rudely interrupted by a flash of white light spreading across his dark brown face.

Propping himself on his elbows, Chance turned and looked in the direction of the light glaring from the house.

The light came from his father's bedroom.

CHAPTER 11

A WILD-EYED O.D. THREW OPEN THE METAL SCREEN DOOR with such force that it quivered uncontrollably on its cookie-sheet thin aluminum frame.

Startled, Chance at first thought he had been too close to the screen door and had been banged up side the head. But feeling no white flash of pain shooting through his skull and hearing no ringing in his ears, Chance realized that he had not been knocked senseless by the door, which meant that the sight standing before him was all too real.

Framed in the narrow doorway, his bulk completely filling the space, O.D. stood 230 pounds of doughy nakedness, stroking an enormous hard-on and bouncing excitedly on ten fat toes. The expansive grin, the top lip curled up tight nearly to the tip of the nose spread taut across his face, revealing a row of white teeth and an inch of purple gum, gave O.D. the look of a bloated, berserk, ballerina.

"Damn man what took you so long? Damn you won't believe this shit man. You won't damn believe it!"

The high-pitched words bumped against each other in their mad rush to get out of O.D.'s mouth.

O.D. didn't respond to the astonished look on his friend's face, if it had even registered with the overly excited young man. O.D. had no time for such observations, he didn't even have time to wait to hear Chance's answer to his question. Before he had even completed his last statement the fat boy had pivoted on his fat toes and took the stairs leading to the basement, two at a time.

"Where's the camera?" O.D. chirped, tossing the question over his round shoulders to Chance, who watched his friend's rusty, jello ass, dance down the steps.

O.D.'s fleshy, flat feet slapped the basement's red speckled brown linoleum tiles with a hollow thud.

"Chance ain't brought the Polaroid," O.D. announced in disappointment to the boys huddled in front of the laundry room entrance, the orange and green tie-dyed sheet hanging from a brass rod, which usually covered the opening pushed to one side of the doorway.

Biggie, like O.D., was buck naked.

Roach had on only a faded green shirt and a pair of white tube socks that drooped around his bird legs.

"Ain't I back up to bat yet?" asked O.D. almost pleading as he kneaded his manhood.

"You a greedy, horny, fat muthafucka ain't you?" spat Biggie in reply.

Chance hadn't moved from the stairwell landing. He was planted at the far end of the basement still trying to make sense of the macabre scene.

When he finally moved toward the doorless entrance to the laundry room, he couldn't determine if he was walking or was being pulled along by some invisible force.

"Don't get no ideas. I'm next," snapped Roach, nudging Chance aside with a bony forearm as he hopped on one wobbly leg kicking off a sock, then switching legs and kicking off the other sock.

"Man you're in my way. I can't see," grumbled O.D., shoving Roach, who threw a half-hearted punch refusing to give ground.

Pushing by Roach and O.D., Biggie swaggered through the tied-dyed sheet that hung limply covering half of the doorway.

Chance moved forward and filled the space vacated by Biggie. He peered into the laundry room, squinting as he tried to adjust to its dimness. Weak sunlight filtered through the small glass block window stuffed high in the brick wall, its white paint flaked in spots revealing red stone.

Framed in a square of pale diffuse light, a pair of sweat-glistened shoulders topping a narrow yellow back were hunched over a multicolored mound of clothes-black socks, white shorts and shirts, blue jeans, green and yellow towels - strewn across the tile floor.

Chance fixed his eyes on X as he humped the pile of dirty clothes, which writhed like snakes on the smooth linoleum. He watched for several seconds before he noticed, one, then two, then several patches of ebony skin peeking out from under the undulating laundry.

Chance followed the patches of skin at either side of X's straining torso. The skin ended in two small feet and a set of red painted toes.

Maybe he had been conked by the screen door, Chance thought to himself, because he still wasn't fully comprehending the scene before him.

"Brotha, brotha, brotha. She got some good shit," sang O.D., still playing with himself, his bloated frame now sprawled out across a plaid couch that was as almost as lumpy as him.

With one tree-trunk leg propped over the wooden arm of the couch, which was scarred with from dozen of cigarette burns, O.D. nursed a bottle of Thunderbird. Letting out a belch, he continued his observations.

"And she got some soft titties. Big ass nipples looking like chocolate M&Ms. Man, I could squeeze those jugs all day," continued O.D. slogging back more wine.

"I wished we could have done her cousin, too, but she upstairs with my big brother and that greedy sucker ain't sharing nothin." O.D. took another long drag of wine.

"I still can't believe this shit. She didn't even want to come." O.D. tipped the neck of the bottle toward the laundry room. "Took her cousin ten minutes to convince her to get in Mike's car with us. All the way over here she kept telling her cousin that they couldn't stay long cus they had to get home before three. But her cousin wasn't hearin' none of that, all hugged up under Mike like she was. Man I thought he was going to crash the way she was all up on him."

Mike was O.D.'s older brother, who was 19, home on leave from the Army and in a few days on his way to the Nam. In the four days he had been home Mike had been with two different chicks, and if O.D. was to be believed, and there was no reason not to believe him, Mike was working on number three. Mike had bragged his first night back home, as he showed off the new 1968 cherry red, fast-back Mustang, to his little brother and his friends, that he intended to "polish me off as much tail as I can. Ain't no bitch in Cleveland safe. Like James Bond say, it's going to be pussy galore. Got's to get while the gettin is good, cus who knows, my ass might get blowed away by some gook or somethin." His words were encased in tiny balls of marijuana smoke and frost that floated on the brisk late afternoon air.

X and Biggie slapped Mike an enthusiastic five, but quickly stuffed their hands back in their pockets to get warm. It might have been a heatwave by February standards in Cleveland, but 40 degrees was still 40 degrees.

However, what sent a chill through O.D. wasn't the temperature, but the last part of his brother's statement. He had tried convincing himself that Mike's being in the Army wasn't a big deal, that his brother didn't necessarily have to end up in the jungle. He could be stationed in Germany with a bunch of white girls, Jayne Mansfield-looking krauts, like the ones their cousin June Bug had written them about last year, which had started Mike thinking about enlisting. Mike believed it when he told O.D. that by joining he would get stationed in some place like Germany.

"If you enlist, the Army let you pick what you want. It's them fools that waits to get drafted that get sent to Nam," Mike had insisted before he headed to the recruiting station six months earlier.

Mike could see his talk about getting blown away had upset O.D., who had completely lost interest in inspecting his brother's new ride. Pinching the joint tight between his fingers he took a long toke and flicked the nub of paper that remained into the bushes.

"Hey, lil bro, I'm just playin'." He barely squeezed out the words between coughing and spitting out tiny fibers of weed that clung to his tongue. "You know nothin' gonna happen to me. I'm one bad dude, it's them slant eyes little yellow cats that better watch out. I'm going to be takin' numbers and kickin' much butt." Mike bear hugged his little brother, who actually was the bigger of the two by 40 pounds and two inches. The playful gesture allowed O.D. to push his fear back in the recesses of his mind.

"We was just cruisin' with Mike, up near the Mount, when Mike peeps this chick he said he knew and pulls over and starts rappin'." O.D.'s attention was equally split between his storytelling and looking over to the laundry room hoping for a sign that it was his turn again.

From what Chance could piece together from O.D.'s disjointed retelling of events, the girl who was now upstairs with Mike had had a crush on the older boy and was flattered that he had even remembered her. The girl's cousin was a reluctant bystander.

After riding around for awhile, Mike had been able to convince the girl under his arm to try some weed, which to everyone's surprise she took to as enthusiastically as Roach and Biggie had four days earlier when Mike produced a joint for his little brother and friends to try. Chance, O.D. and X declined. Roach claimed he had previous experience with weed. Not to be shown up by Roach, Biggie said he had even copped a nickel bag a couple of months earlier.

"The other chick tried to pretend she was down. But I could tell she was getting nervous. I think she was scared the police was gonna to pull us over. So when Mike stopped by the crib she couldn't wait to get out of the ride," O.D. continued, raising from the couch and filling the laundry room opening.

"Anyway, we all comes downstairs and start playing dirty hearts, you know if you lose you have to take a drink. The one with my brother was game but your friend wanted to go, but her cousin teased her about being a square."

"My friend? What you mean my friend?"

O.D. ignored Chance's question and continued the story.

"We all had a few drinks. Mixed some of my daddy's Gordon's gin in with the Rose, man that was some good shit. Anyway, after a few hands of dirty hearts she wants to go." O.D. angled his head toward the pile of clothes.

"She starts sniffling and all, telling her cousin they got to go. So Mike tells her she can't go home drunk and he goes up and brings her back a cup of tea to sober her up. Then Mike and the other chick split upstairs.

"She sips the tea and starts to calm down." O.D. took a sip of wine.

"Biggie got his arm around her talking about she be alright and that he'll walk her home all the while trying to feel up her tits and kiss her. She was pushing him away at first but then it must have gotten good to her because she just stopped. Dropped the damn cup and broke it though. One of my mom's good cups, too.

"She just lets Biggie kiss her for awhile then he takes off her shirt. Then next thing you know they getting it on right there on the couch. Man, when we helped Biggie move her into the laundry room I got little scared, she wasn't moving much. Biggie talking 'bout he knocked her out with his strokin'. Probably just couldn't handle the drinking." An expansive, gum showing, grin spread across O.D.'s moon face again, but this time there was a sinister curve to the lips.

"Who you talking bout?" Chance asked again.

"Tellin' you we could've had a real orgy up in here if my brother was willing to share." O.D. ignored Chance's question, purposely trying to irritate him.

Refusing to let the fat boy know that he had succeeded in doing just that, Chance, returned his eyes to X and the pile of laundry.

It took all that he had to fight the urge to rush to the pile of clothing. Not that he wanted to put a halt to what was happening, but to simply satisfy his curiosity.

He wanted to rummage madly through the pile of clothes to uncover who O.D. was talking about.

"Go! Go! Go!" The wine and lust fueled chant filled the room and crowded out Chance's thoughts.

Suddenly X went rigid, gave a deep raspy grunt, shuddered and then flopped over on his back, a blue sock plastered to his chest.

Before O.D. could move, Roach dove into the pile of clothes and was soon adrift in a churning sea of colored fabric.

"Hey," stammered O.D., not understanding how Roach had shot past him.

"You snooze you lose," said X as he pushed himself up out of the mound of clothes and tugged the wine bottle from O.D.'s hand. X staggered through the doorway, smacked the tie-dyed sheet aside and sank into the couch.

If it weren't for the one motionless, midnight leg peeking out at various points-a square of thigh and a sliver of knee and the entire lower portion from calf to toes—Roach could have easily been alone in the pile of musty clothing.

Roach pounded his body into the mound of laundry again and again, grunting louder with every violent thrust.

Chance felt himself straining against the rough metal zipper of his pants as he watched Roach's backside rise and fall.

Roach's animal grunts pushed the walls of the basement in on Chance.

Jose Feliciano hiccupped "*Come on baby light, baby light, baby light...*" from the record skipping on the hi-fi.

Chance felt trapped. The room was burning up. He skimmed sweat from his face with the flat of his hand. He wanted to throw open a window. He wanted to run but he wasn't sure in which direction.

"Man, hurry up Roach, and let me get back on the train. Whooo, whooo!" O.D. pretended to pull the chain of a train whistle.

Roach growled at the top of his lungs and then collapsed into a panting heap, his face buried to his ears in dirty laundry.

That's when Chance saw them a pair of large almond shaped eyes. Eyes so dark that they looked like they were studded with two great black lumps of coal.

The eyes were familiar to him, yet they were different. The eyes Chance had known were full of life and disarming in their warmth.

These eyes, staring out from the pile of clothes, were vacant. There was no longer a person named Mavis residing in them.

These eyes, without a hint of recognition in them, stared up through the worn floor joists, which were spaced like railroad ties along the ceiling of the basement.

Then the eyes turned on Chance.

He watched as the heavy lids slid close and a stream of tears melted across ebony cheeks.

In that moment, while Mavis' eyes were pressed shut, Chance felt that he could have escaped. He had even told himself to go, but before his muscles could answer the command of his brain, the dark eyes flashed open.

This time a panicky Mavis was there in those eyes.

"Get up off it," hissed Biggie. There was such evil intent in his voice that the room that had seemed so full of noise just moments ago was now silent.

Normally, Roach would have stood up to Biggie, he never wanting to be seen playing the punk. Roach had stood up on more than a few occasions to boys twice his size. Once he had even taken on the Florence brothers, all four of them, and had given as good as he received. But Roach also sensed the murderous ring in Biggie's words, so he quietly rolled off of Mavis and squeezed up against the washing machine.

"Let me show you faggots how it's done," said Biggie, reaching between his thighs for his weapon.

He stabbed himself deep into Mavis. Her limp body passively took his attack.

Biggie ground rough, callused hands over her breasts and gnawed at her neck and shoulders as he slammed into her again and again.

Chance could feel Mavis desperately clinging to him with those almond shaped eyes. She had grabbed hold to Chance with those eyes, pleading with him, begging him to do something.

"What does she want from me?" thought Chance and he silently cursed Mavis for putting him in this predicament. He wondered how Mavis could have done this to him. Hadn't they been getting close during the last few months, sharing late night conversations on the phone and passing notes to one another in study hall?

And then there were those encounters in the hallways between classes. Nothing special, just a wink or a nod, Chance always careful to be discreet, still concerned by what his boys might say if they say him making eyes at that "coal black gal."

Just a few days ago he had met Mavis at one of her babysitting gigs. They had kissed and felt each other up, she worried that the family she was sitting for would be coming home at anytime. He hadn't even gotten mad when she said that they had better stop before they went too far and he stopped.

He had even apologized to her about how he had treated her after that slow dance at that party months earlier. And now, after all that he had done for her, she was down here in O.D.'s basement giving it up like a $2 hoe.

He would never forgive her for being in that basement. He would never forgive her for being so stupid, so, so, whorish.

In his mind Chance screamed "Hoe. Hoe. Stupid hoe!"

Why wouldn't she let him alone? Why wouldn't she just stop looking at him?

Chance tried to focus his thoughts, tried to mentally command Mavis to let him go, but she just kept on staring up at him, kept on holding tight to him.

Just when Chance thought he would explode from the voices rumbling in his head, he sensed that Mavis' grip had loosened. He was able to free his eyes from her's and look at Biggie still lurching violently over her body. With every thrust the fixed stare of her eyes became less intense. Her eyes fluttered, and then finally shut. When they reopened Mavis had gone and the large vacant black eyes once again gazed up into the floor beams above.

Free of Mavis' demands Chance cursed her for being in that basement. He told himself that she was in that laundry room because she was a slut. He tried to convince himself that only a trampy, hoe would let herself be in such a situation.

That's what Chance wanted desperately to believe. But he knew better.

He knew there was no reason for Mavis to have feared these boys in the basement. She went to school with them and had known them, at least in passing, for years. O.D. had even sung in the Mt. Zion First Baptist church choir with her before he stopped going to church regularly a few years back when the fellas started teasing him, calling him "preacher boy."

Chance wanted to be angry with Mavis. He wanted to blame her. He wanted, needed this to be all her fault.

"Man, I know you done had some of that pussy before. I can't believe you would hold out on your boys like that."

O.D.'s stupid words pulled Chance out of his thoughts. He felt the fat boy's hand on his shoulder.

"Fuck you!" The words exploded from deep inside Chance.

He knocked the oppressive hand from his shoulder and shoved its owner hard against the wall.

"What's the hell matter with you?" coughed O.D. Chance was half-way up the stairs before O.D. regained his balance.

"Check it out. The boy's leaving," said O.D. turning to the others.

The laughter coming from the basement bounced off Chance's back as he stiff-armed the screen door and bolted out of the house.

It was a good two weeks before Chance started coming back around Biggie, O.D. and the others. He had vowed to stay away from them for good. Vowed to stay away because he was mad with them, mad with Mavis and mad at himself.

Eventually, things returned to normal for Chance, helped by the fact that he hadn't seen Mavis. At first he was relieved that he hadn't noticed her in school for the first several days after the basement incident, but later became concerned when days stretched into weeks. He later learned from her cousin Bernadette that her parents had sent her to live with her grandmother in Kentucky.

There would be several times in the years to come that Chance would consider talking about what happened in the basement. He wanted to know if Mavis' eyes haunted his friends like they did him. He wanted to know, but he never asked.

"Say it loud, I'm black and I'm proud.
I said say it loud, I'm black and I'm proud..."
James Brown, 1968-1970

CHAPTER 12

IT SEEMED TO CHANCE THAT HE HAD BEEN SITTING in the same spot for days, stuck in a space that straddled reality and dreams, in a shadowy realm between the real and unreal.

He was fairly sure that he had gone through all the motions of his everyday life for the last two days waking up, going to school, going to track practice, coming home, doing homework, eating dinner, going to bed. Yet, he couldn't be sure.

Maybe he had been in the half light of the basement for all that time maybe forever? It wasn't beyond reason, because of the totally unreasonableness of the last 48 hours, to think that he and his friends had just sprouted from of the basement's cold brown linoleum tiles.

The light flickered sporadically, undulating in a blue-gray glow that ricocheted off the motionless boys planted in a tight semi-circle in front of a television set.

The dull illumination danced on and around shoulders and heads, splashing the silhouetted figures in varying shades of gray light, which seemed to throb and shift, continuously growing and then receding in intensity.

The surreal light radiated out from the television's round screen that framed flat, miniature images.

"Chet, can you hear me? What can you tell our viewers about the funeral preparations?" The questions came from a tiny, gray man seated behind a desk, his tiny, shallow voice coming from the TV's cloth-covered speakers.

"At this moment, details are still sketchy. Certainly, the nation's dignitaries, political, civil rights, and religious leaders will all be in attendance Tuesday in Atlanta to honor Dr. King," came the reply from a different tiny, shallow voice. Then a close-up of a white man holding a microphone to his face nearly filled the entire screen.

"This is one of the darkest events in the history of this nation. And, I must tell you, everywhere I go, the grief of this country and her people is clearly evident..."

"Turn that shit off. I don't want to hear no more. That's all that anybody's been talking about for the last two days and all this talk don't change one goddamn thing," spat Biggie, slapping at the basement's darkness in disgust as he rose to his feet.

"It ain't like them muthafuckas care. Hell, I bet if the truth be told them crackers on TV is glad that someone offed Dr. King. I'm sick of all this sad mouth phony shit," Biggie continued, his words directed to the back of Afros as all four sets of eyes were glued to the television.

The white men framed by the 18-inch lighted circle continued their diatribe, reporting on the "unwarranted and senseless wave of violence" engulfing many of the nation's cities.

"It is a shame that the Negro apostle of non violence is having his memory marred by the mindless rioting playing out in the streets of a number of American cities. Rioting in Chicago has already claimed at least 19 victims and the fires are still burning in Newark, Washington D.C., Pittsburgh, Boston, Cincinnati, Nashville, and in countless smaller towns," said the shrunken white man in a monotone clip.

"President Johnson has asked Americans, particularly those in the inner city to deny violence its victory. And words urging calm have come from responsible Negro leaders across the country...."

"Give me some of that wine," snapped Biggie, reaching down for the bottle at O.D.'s side.

"Be cool. You want my moms to hear," whispered Chance.

"Be cool? Be cool? What's wrong, mamma's boy? You scared she gonna find out we down here drinking and going to take a switch to your backside?" Biggie shot back, his voice growing louder. Placing a hand on his narrow hips, he threw back his head and swallowed the red liquid in big gulps sending waves of warmth through his chest.

"Man, what's with you, Biggie? Shit, why you got to always be an asshole," said Roach, bending over to turn up the volume on the television, hoping it would drown out Biggie's voice.

"Chance's Mom's gonna come down here and bust us all then all your mammies and pappies gonna have something for your asses when you gets home," added O.D, trying unsuccessfully to lighten the tense moment.

"Fuck all you mama's boys. I don't want no punk ass mamma's boys wid me tonight," growled Biggie, deliberately exaggerating the words.

"White folks crazy." There wasn't a trace of judgment in X's hushed voice. The words were spoken in a flat tone and very matter of factly.

The words had caught the other boys by surprise. They had almost forgotten that X was in the basement. Usually the volatile one, X, ever ready with a crack that always seemed to hit home and hit deep, had earned his rep by running his mouth. He had become almost invisible in his unusual silence of the past 48 hours.

"White folks crazy," X said again in a voice a bit louder, but still devoid of emotion.

"My grandma ain't stopped crying since she heard the news. She just sits and rocks and asks the lawd to have mercy," O.D. offered, trying to lift the strange spell that X was under; it made him feel uneasy. The pudgy boy had hoped that offering his grandmother up as an easy target of ridicule would bring back the X they knew.

Ordinarily, an opportunity to take pot shots at anyone's mother, or grandmother, particularly Berta Jean, O.D.'s countrified, buck tooth, slew foot, grandmama would have immediately lit a match to X's explosive tongue. He would have rained torrents of insults on the comical Berta Jean, like the master dozens player he was. But, for the last two day's X had dried up. If he had been feeling sorrow, anger or grief about the assassination of Dr. King, it had all drained out of him.

"Crackers do whatever they want to do and I'm tired of that shit," said Biggie, getting back on his soap box.

"They blow up little girls in churches, lynch young boys for thinking bout looking at a white bitch. They kick our asses, sic dogs on us, use us for target practice and they can't understand it when we explode and burn down shit."

O.D. offered that the rioting, which had burned out blocks in Washington, Pittsburgh, Chicago and even Cincinnati "ain't what Dr. King would have wanted. For us to be doing all this burning and looting is against everything the man stood for."

"Fuck you, O.D. You sound jus like them cracker newsmen or one of them Uncle Tom preachers," Biggie spat back in reply.

"All I know is that I'm proud black folk ain't cutting no fool here, burning down where we live 'cause we mad at white folks," said O.D.

"Didn't I tell y'all that nigga was an Uncle Tom. Come on out here, Tom, and do a little tap dance for massuh," Biggie said. "I ain't no damn Tom."

"Yes, you is boy. Your Tom ass always skinning and grinning round them honkey teachers at school. Now, tell me ain't I right?"

"Why don't you just shut up, Biggie? You ain't the only one hurting," Chance barked.

"I may be hurting but I ain't no pussy like you punks. Man, give me that damn bottle," said Biggie glaring at O.D.

"Fool, the bottle's empty."

"I ain't asked you that. I said give me the god damn bottle."

Biggie snatched the bottle from O.D. and turned it straight up to the ceiling just above his tongue, which snaked between yellow teeth. He waited a full 30 seconds before one then another drop of red liquid seeped from the bottle.

"Let's get the hell out of here. Listening to this shit on TV is working my last nerve," said Biggie. He didn't wait to see if anyone was following him up the stairs and out the side door.

Chance was relieved by Biggie's exit. He had visions of his mother materializing in the basement at any moment.

"Let's hat up," Chance said, rising to click off the television. The TV crackled loudly as the round screen glowed almost white, then slowly darkened. The white circle of light shrank under the press of blackness coming in from the edges of the screen, flared to a pin point and then disappeared.

Chance followed his friends as they trudged up the stairs and out the door, pulling it shut behind him.

"Where are you going, young man?" The disembodied voice came from Chance's mother somewhere in the house.

"Nowhere, mom, just down to Biggie's, I mean Julian's house."

"Well, you make sure that's the only place you go and be back here no later than nine. There's just too much happening. Just too much happening."

Chance stood at the door and silently nodded his head.

"Did you hear me, boy?"

"Yes, ma'am."

"Well, answer me then. There is just too much happening out there and you don't need to be out and about."

"Mom, ain't nothing going to..."

"You heard me. I don't want you off of this street." Mrs. Marshall's voice cut her son off in mid-sentence.

"Yeah, okay mom. Later."

The side door closed with a thud, followed by the tinny clang of the aluminum screen.

The basketball banged hard against the rusted, perforated metal backboard and then swirled along the circumference of the rim three times before dropping down through the torn net.

Chance grabbed the ball as it bounced off the blacktop and flung it back to O.D., who immediately rattled in another jumper from the top of the key.

"The shit makes you mad. I mean they fuck with you, constantly killing off your leaders, tell you what you can and can't do, forever hassling your black ass and then they expect you to just take all their shit and smile. Fuck that," said Chance, his words punctuated by the hollow thud of the ball he bounced between his legs.

The basketball again snapped the net and came down hard on the hood of the lime green Chevy Impala. The noise startled X who sat alone in the car, his hands stuffed deep into the pouch at the front of his hooded sweatshirt.

"Man, stop hitting my car," complained Biggie, bending his face down to the hood and running his hand across its metal skin, inspecting for damage.

"If my hood is dented, that's your ass."

"Ain't nobody told you to park that damn Model T push-mobile up under the basket," Roach roared, unleashing a flood of laughter.

It felt good for them to laugh, if only for a few seconds.

"I'm hatting-up and if any you chumps wanta ride in my Model T, rather than humping on home on shoe leather, you besta get in."

Biggie pulled a red rabbit's foot key chain from his shirt pocket and scooted behind the steering wheel. He willed the Impala to life with a twist of the rabbit's foot.

The motor coughed several times, and burped a white puff of smoke, before finding its deep growl.

O.D. ducked quickly between X and Roach and dived into the back seat head first to secure a window.

The move by O.D. sparked a pushing and shoving match between Chance and Roach, both boys determined to get the other rear seat window.

Roach got Chance into a head lock and tossed him playfully toward the back of the car. Before Chance could regain his balance, Roach had jumped in the Impala and slammed the car door shut.

O.D. splayed his big arms out of the window of his door and bolted himself in place, his elbows pressed tight against the door's outside edge, just in case Chance planned a sneak attack on his side of the car.

Chance stood helpless outside the car not believing he had been outmaneuvered. Biggie and X at the windows in the front seat and Roach and O.D. at the windows in the back. There was no way around it Chance was going to have to squeeze in between Roach and O.D. or Biggie and X, either way he was riding bitch, the ultimate affront to his manhood.

He thought about charging Roach one more time, maybe catching him unexpectedly and yanking him out of the car, or body slamming him, lowering a shoulder to shove him in the middle seat. But when Chance looked at Roach sizing up his chances of a surprise attack, he could see that Roach was ready for him.

Maybe he would bum rush X, thought Chance, after all X was in such a weird mood there might be the possibility of getting the upper hand and gangstering the window seat away from him. Chance knew it was a crazy gamble challenging X, particularly when it came to car seating assignments.

Chance knew that X, probably more than the rest of them, considered riding bitch tantamount to being labeled a fag. Not for as long as Chance had known X, had his friend ever sat wedged in between two hard legs in the middle of a car seat. When he was only ten, X had actually duked it out with Eddie Clayborne because he refused to sit in the middle.

Obviously, it hadn't mattered to X that Clayborne, who was at the time 14 and had a well deserved tough guy reputation, because X didn't hesitate to sucker punch the older boy dead in his mouth. And although the attack caught Clayborne by surprise, and the blood trickling down his chin seemed to daze him, the bigger boy quickly recovered and then proceeded to whip X like he owned him.

Chance had been too terrified for his own safety to come to X's aid because even two against one when it came to tussling with Clayborne were long odds. All Chance could do was pray that Mr. Robinson, the Boy Scout leader, would hurry up and get to the car. It seemed to take Mr. Robinson forever to arrive. When he finally got there, he had to struggle mightily for several minutes to pull Clayborne off of X, who to everyone's amazement was still more than willing to continuing scrapping despite the dozen knots that had risen on his head.

Even when Mr. Robinson threatened not to take him to the Indian's baseball game unless he got in the car that "very minute and next to me." X, bruised and bloodied, still refused to sit in the middle. He defiantly shook his knotted head "no", slammed the car door, and limped home.

Unfortunately, Chance had found himself in the embarrassing position in the middle seat more than a few times and he detested it. He never seemed to be able to find the right face-saving comebacks to the insults heaped unmercifully on the occupant of the bitch seat.

So, Chance was caught totally off guard when X, without looking up, simply slid a few inches to his left to make room for Chance to sit.

Chance hesitated and tried to size-up the situation. Even when he finally sat down next to the window, Chance was uncomfortably and tense as he considered the possibilities. He readied himself to be shoved out the door by X with a swift kick or a flurry of punches, but when after a few breathless moments the attack didn't come, Chance slowly swung the passenger door shut.

"Are you in the damn car yet?" Biggie stomped down on the accelerator not waiting for an answer.

The Impala's rear wheels squealed loudly as ringlets of smoke rose from the asphalt.

Biggie twisted the steering wheel hard to the left, sending the car into a 180 degree spin until the front bumper was pointed out of the playground. The moon hubs on the rear tires spun wildly, catching the yellow light from the street lamps and reflected it back into the night in a thousand sparks.

"Hit the radio, X. Get us some tunes up in this bad boy," commanded O.D., as he danced in his seat and slapped some skin to Roach.

X didn't move.

"Yo, X, you heard me, flip on the tunes. Get on your J-O-B my man," said O.D., knowing full well that the rules of the bitch seat required X to operate the lighter, which didn't work in the Impala, along with the radio.

"This ain't no party brother, so we ain't having no music," said X.

"Is this your car, man?" asked O.D., leaning up behind the driver's seat.

"Hey, Big, you gonna let him tell you what you can and can't do in your car? I wouldn't stand for that shit, man," O.D. continued.

Biggie glanced over at X. The look on the boy's thin yellow face dissuaded him from asserting his right of ownership. Instead he turned on O.D.

"Don't be worrying about my radio. Just be sure your always broke ass got some ducats to pitch in for the wine."

"Be cool man. I was jus messin' with him," said O.D.

Be cool? X wondered how he could possibly "be cool." He hadn't known how to be cool since he first head the news about Dr. King being gunned down on the balcony of a Memphis motel. Like his friends, like everyone black, X was hurt, shocked and grief stricken, but for some reason he had this feeling that his pain went deeper, and he wasn't sure why. He hadn't particularly been an avid admirer of King and the civil rights movement. X remembered that his mother always felt uncomfortable when the marches and demonstrations were on the news. His mother, if she didn't turn off the TV in disgust, would rock slowly on the couch, her arms hugged tight across her flat chest, and complain "We ain't going to get nothing trying to force ourselves on white folks. All this ruckus just going to make it harder on colored people."

X always felt a bit ashamed that his mother came off like such a Tom, but she made it a point to make sure "her family," which meant him and Mr. Johnson, wasn't involved in "no racial mess."

A few years back, when black folks in Cleveland were up in arms about the discriminatory practices of the Cleveland schools, X's mother almost had a nervous breakdown, especially after a white minister, who was part of the protest demonstration against the building of anymore segregated schools, was run over and killed by a bulldozer at a school construction site. When Negro parents across the city decided to keep the pressure on by a one-day-boycott, keeping their children home from school, or sending them to freedom schools set up in the basement of several churches, his mother made sure she sent X to school.

X and about 15 other kids were given special ribbons by big-eared Mrs. Thoreson, the principal of Elliot Junior High, for showing their "commitment to education" and attending school the day of the boycott.

X's red ribbon was hung proudly in a gold-toned frame right under the picture of Jesus at the head of his mother's bed.

That was why X had a hard time trying to make sense of the physical pain he felt and was still feeling when he heard Dr. King had been assassinated. It was a very real gnawing in his guts. It was like a bunch of hunger-crazed rats were eating their way through his body, chewing a path from his chest to his bowels.

"I'm going to fuck me somebody up tonight," screamed Biggie, leaning his head out of the window. "I'm going to fuck up some cracker."

"Yeah, that makes a lot of sense. That's going to change everything," said Chance dismissing Biggie's outburst with a wave of his hand.

"That's right, chump. It's going to change something. It's going to change how I'm feeling. It's going to make me feel good to know that somebody white is going to pay for the shit they done and been doing to us forever. I'm going to feel damn good." Biggie slammed the flat of his palms against the steering wheel for emphasis.

"Take my ass home," said O.D., a little worried.

"What? Do my ears deceive me? Tell me it ain't you trying to punk out O.D. I would have expected that pie-back shit from Chance or Roach, but not you O.D.," said Biggie mockingly.

"Man, Biggie, stop talkin' stupid. You done drunk too much wine," said Chance.

"Stupid? Who you calling stupid, punk? You hear that X? I'm stupid and I'm drunk."

X didn't respond to Biggie, who was becoming more animated and loud, flailing his hands so much that the car swerved across the center line of the road several times.

"Biggie, you ain't going to do nothing but run off at the mouth like you always do. So why don't you give everybody a break and just shut up." The irritation and frustration were clear in Chance's voice.

"Nothing? I show y'all pussies nothing."

Biggie slammed his right foot hard to the floor sending the car skidding down the street in a screech of rubber.

"All you punks got to do is to keep an eye out for the cops and I'll do the rest."

"Damn, Biggie, stop being stupid and slow this car down."

"Yeah, man, cool out before you kill us all up in here," stammered O.D., really frightened now.

The Impala roared up behind, and then passed, a blue and white station wagon. The woman behind the wheel was so rattled that she pulled quickly toward the curb and slowed almost to a stop.

"Was that a white hoe in that car? asked Biggie, his yellow eyes narrowing as a demented grin widened his mouth. He pulled to the curb, doused all but the parking lights, and idled the Impala.

"Whatcha going to do? Just leave that lady alone." O.D.'s pleas were joined by Chance and Roach.

If the white woman had noticed the red taillights standing still ahead of her, she didn't act like it. Apparently recovered, she pulled away from the curb and proceeded at the same slow pace along her previous course.

The boys turned around and stared out the back window, Biggie in agitated anticipation, and the others in deep concern as they watched the station wagon approach. Only X seemed unfazed. He hadn't turned around with the others to look out the back window, instead his stare remained fixed, totally absorbed by the nearly imperceptible gyrations of the silver peace medallion that hung from a chain on the rearview mirror just inches from his nose.

"Damn, why don't that crazy bitch make a U-turn," whispered Chance under his breath. It didn't make sense to him that the woman, after being nearly forced off the road, would keep on coming. Hadn't she seen them pull over? Could she be that stupid?

The station wagon's head lamps kept coming, growing brighter and larger as the car approached.

The white light splashed along the back and side of the Impala, as the station wagon slowly passed and then began to shrink in the distance.

O.D. dropped a ham hock hand on Biggie's shoulder and squeezed. The gesture was one last plea to let the woman alone.

Biggie shrugged off the imposing paw and moved the Impala from the curb until it settled into the pull of the station wagon's fading tail lights.

The red needle at the center of the speedometer, which glowed blue-green in the darkened cockpit of the Impala, ticked passed 40, 50, 60, then trembled as it strained to touch 70.

The red tail lights of the station wagon were rapidly reeled in by the Impala. Seconds before the cars' bumpers collided, Biggie yanked on the high beams and laid on the horn.

"Whaaaaaaaaaaaaa!!" The Impala's horn blared as Biggie veered to the left of the station wagon, which quickly receded in the rearview mirror.

"Did you see that shit? I scared the shit out of that bitch," announced Biggie triumphantly, as he slammed the flat of his palms against the steering wheel and cackled in laughter.

"Damn, Biggie why you do some shit like that?" yelled Roach.

"'Cause I wanted to and 'cause I could," said Biggie as he ducked the car down a side street.

"Fuck that white bitch anyway. She got what she deserved. Riding up in our neighborhood like she owns the muthafucking street. I showed her that she don't own shit round here."

"Man, she was driving down the street minding her own business. She wasn't bothering nobody," Chance complained.

"So, what the fuck? You want me to shed tears for that bitch? Hell, we was minding our own business a couple weeks ago when them honky cops stopped us up in Beachwood. All up in our face asking us what we doing in their part of town. Or did you forget that shit? Them cops followed us right out of town. You tell me why they did that?"

Chance didn't speak and when he didn't Biggie continued his lecture.

"Hell, in Murray Hill they be kicking black folks asses all the time just for coming through they neighborhood."

"Remember last year when they almost killed that African student from the university at the laundromat?" added O.D.

"That's right. Damn university two blocks from Murray Hill and college kids up there all the time. Damn black man goes to wash his dirty draws and they try to kill him. Stuffed his jungle ass in a dryer," Biggie said.

"I'm telling you, all white folks the same. All of them just like them crazy wops up in Murray Hill."

"Then Murray Hill is where you need to go instead of messing around with some little old white lady." There was no emotion in X's voice. It was just an observation spoken matter of factly.

The statement stunned the car into silence and drained all of Biggie's newly won bravado from him, but just momentarily.

"Yeah. I like that. Let's go fuck with them wops in Murray Hill." Biggie played bad, but his too high voice betrayed him.

"You all must be crazy. I ain't going down to no Murray Hill," whined O.D.

Chance and Roach shared O.D.'s sentiments, but they refused to give voice to their fears. Biggie was just as scared as the rest of them, but he seemed incapable at times of stopping his mouth from writing checks that he knew his ass couldn't cash.

"I'm down with you X. Check it out, Murray Hill Muthafuckas, here we come," yelled Biggie, jamming his head out the window to holler at the stars.

After the initial wave of macho had washed over Biggie and receded, he pulled himself back through the window and sat silent behind the wheel as he let the prospect of rolling through Murray Hill slowly sink in. He pulled the Impala to the curb and parked.

"Well?"

"Well what? asked Biggie, turning to X who continued to stare impassively at the peace medallion. He didn't look at Biggie when he answered.

"Well, my brother, are you going to turn this hunk of junk around and get us started on our journey?"

"Just what are we supposed to do. I mean what's the plan?" asked Biggie, wishing now that he had just shut up.

The word "plan" seemed so out of place to Chance. Since when did anybody need to a plan to do something totally stupid, completely devoid of any sort of logic.

Yet, as crazy as he knew it was, there was something about driving through Murray Hill that appealed to him. Chance had no more idea than the rest of his friends, what they would do once they hit Murray Hill. Maybe they would yell obscenities out the window, or throw an empty wine bottle at a window. All Chance knew was that he wanted to defy the unspoken rules that he seemed to always be bumping up against. He wanted to do something to them to let them know that he was tired of their shit.

Chance was sick of them, with their featureless pale faces, floating around the edges of his life, making decisions about where Negroes could go, what Negroes could do, how Negroes should act, and even where they were allowed to reach.

He was tired of his world being circumscribed by them, as they sat watching, deciding when, where and how they were going to mess with you, how they were going to insert themselves in your life.

On a whim, maybe they would decide to pour sugar on your nappy head for sitting at a lunch counter.

Or maybe they would decide to beat and lynch you, like they did that Emmett Till, because they decide you ain't allowed to smile at a white woman.

In an old Jet Magazine photo, Till, lay in a coffin, his head swollen to the size of a basketball, his stitched-together face resembling nothing human even after its reconstruction, flashed through Chance's mind. The dead boys picture was followed by other images that bubbled-up, one after another from Chance's memory. They were pictures he had seen in Jet, and Ebony and in the Negro history books that both his grandmother's collected, pictures of bombed out churches, burned buses, black men hanging from trees, and slaves, men and women, who had puffy keloid-scares on their backs that looked like creeping vines, sending out tentacles in every direction.

"Or maybe they tell you that you ain't good enough to see Tarzan."

"What?" asked O.D.

It took Chance a few moments to realize that he had spoken his last thoughts out loud.

"Oh, nothing man. Just skip it."

O.D. hearing the embarrassment in Chance's voice didn't press for an explanation.

"Let's get going if we going," said Chance, who now found the idea of driving through Murray Hill very appealing.

"Let's stop and get us another taste before we go," said O.D., not really sure if he had made the suggestion to get more wine hoping the alcohol would bolster his nerve to go to Murray Hill, or to fortify him so he could defy his friends by getting out of the car and walking home.

Before O.D. could contemplate the question further, Biggie had turned around and slapped him five.

"Man, O.D., you done finally said something tonight that makes some sense." With that, the Impala pulled from the curb and headed out, back down Harvard Avenue.

The Impala, lights turned off, purred in the square of darkness provided by the broken street lamp at the rear of Mike's, the last example of a mom and pop's store still left in their neighborhood.

Mickolo Malinski, who everyone called Mike, had been doing business in the same red-brick store since 1941, when the Lee Harvard neighborhood was still ethnic Poles, Hungarians, Slavs, a few Jews and a handful of Italians.

Mike, who now ran the store with his son, Little Mike, was one of the few white business owners who didn't move out in the late 50s when the neighborhood turned black, almost overnight. Now, most of the business were still white-owned, but none of the owners still lived in the neighborhood. But Mike and Little Mike, lived with their families, nine people in all, in the two apartments that occupied the second story of the storefront grocery.

"Listen what I say; people are people, white, colored, whatever. As long they pay me grocery bill, I'm happy man." Mickolo was famous for that refrain. The big, red-faced, oil-drum of a man, who was never without a butcher's apron, which couldn't accommodate his massive torso, had a way with people. Everyone liked Mickolo, probably because he liked everyone.

At one time or another just about every boy in the neighborhood had been employed by Mickolo and his son. Both Biggie and O.D. worked for them, cleaning the storeroom and restocking the shelves two nights a week.

Now, the pay wasn't great. "You trying to bankruptcy me?" was Mickolo's other famous line. But Biggie and O.D. weren't working simply for the salary, but the fringe benefits, which they carried out to the dumpster inside empty boxes, at least once a week.

"Fringes, my man, fringes," announced O.D., holding up the second of three bottles of Wild Irish Rose, he had just liberated from the dumpster. Light laughter drifted through the Impala as several dark hands reached the wine.

None of the hands belonged to X. His hands, balled in fists, remained stuffed deep inside the pouch of his sweatshirt, his gaze fixed on the peace symbol.

The laughter in the car grew louder as the wine worked its magic.

The Impala's head lamps came to life, pouring out in two separate beams that eventually came together in a pool of white light 10 feet in front of the car.

Biggie ratcheted the car into drive and crept away from the side of the grocery store.

Chance closed his eyes and breathed deeply of the cool rushing in through the wide-open windows. The high-pitched whine, which came is short bursts as the Impala rode past parked cars soon became one long drone as the car picked up speed.

It wasn't until the Impala came to a stop that Chance realized that he had dozed off. It took him another few minutes for him to revive enough to make out the car had stopped at the top of Murray Hill.

Looking out the dirty windshield and down the hill, Chance could clearly make out the five blocks of small storefronts, the three Catholic churches, and the rows of clapboard houses that made up Murray Hill.

The Impala's idling engine, that had been barely audible before, now roared in his ears. Chance became aware of the distinct sensation of the passenger compartment shrinking.

"Shit, man, shit." O.D. repeated like a chant, as he nervously kneaded the sides of his face between his fat, sweaty hands.

Chance wanted the car to turn around and head back home, and he knew he wasn't alone in that desire. But, he also knew that he, nor anyone else in the car was going to suggest retreat.

Biggie sat frozen, both hands clutched tight on the steering wheel.

Roach, who had finished off the third bottle of wine all by himself, and was on another plane of reality shouted—"let's head'em-up and move' em out." The words amused him so that he doubled over in a convulsion of laughter. In his near epileptic state, Roach attempted to slap five to O.D., who disgustedly pushed him away.

"Man, this shit ain't funny," spat O.D.

"Head em up and move' em out," Roach yelled again, guffawing so much that he all but choked on the words.

Biggie seemed to be in a trance, his movements were zombie-like as he pressed firmly down on the gas pedal.

When the car started its long descent, Biggie came back to himself. Four pair of wide eyes flashed at one another. Chance, sensing the shared panic, and not wanting to risk someone blurting out a plan the might prove more dangerous than his, swallowed what spit he could gather and pulled himself together enough to speak.

"OK. Check it out. We just going to be cool. Just cruise through nice and slow. Let these dago muthafuckas know we ain't afraid of their punk asses. We ain't got to put on no show. We just got to maintain our cool and dare them to say anything to us."

"Ridin' slow and ridin' low," blurted out Roach, which sent him into spasm of laughter again.

Biggie, anxious to grab onto the life line tossed by Chance, seconded the suggestion.

"Yeah, we going to slide right on down the main drag like we own it. Gangster leaning all the way," said Biggie slouching down in his seat, just the wrist of his left hand resting on top of the steering wheel, his right hand cupped under his chin.

The carload of black boys traveled unnoticed for the first three blocks. And, if any of the boys had diverted their eyes slightly from their straight ahead gazes, they would have noticed that there were very few people on the street. They would have seen the two elderly woman, both slumped under heavy shawls, pushing identical rickety, metal grocery carts.

The boys would have noticed the two dark-haired kids, winter coats tied around their waists, racing from the closed bakery and up the steps of St. Francis of Assisi, where three middle-aged men sat in deep conversation.

"Only two more blocks to go," O.D. said expectantly under his breath.

It wasn't until the Impala inched by Momma Rosa's Pizzeria that its passengers were spotted.

The three teens coming out of the glass doors of the pizza shop shot quizzical looks at each other. They seem to be having a hard time believing their eyes.

Chance was even more shocked than the three Italian teens had been when he realized the Impala had come to a complete stop.

"Go through the damn light. Biggie, go through the light," urged Chance, his words forcing their way through clenched teeth.

"It's red. The light's red."

"So what. Go through, the fucking light," barked O.D.

"I can't, the damn lights red," said Biggie, pleading for understanding.

"Shit man, shit," chanted O.D., which set Roach on a laughing jag once again.

"Niggers. Get your black monkey asses out of here," yelled the tallest of the white boys, as he tossed his leather jacket to the steps of the pizzeria.

"Fuck you wa-, wa-, wops," Roach shouted back.

The white boys couldn't make out the words, which had gotten lost in Roach's laughter.

Chance's eyes darted up and down the lamp-lighted street. But no one was coming out of the shadows to join the fray.

O.D. beat frantically at the back of Biggie's seat, begging him to run the light.

"Fuck you, you black spear-chucking jungle bunnies."

The men on the church steps finally looked up from the conversation but remained seated.

"Suck my big dick, cracker," shouted Roach again, who was the only one in the car keeping up his end of the ritual.

The light finally flashed green. The Impala leapt forward.

The white boys, realizing the carload of blacks was moving, found the courage to come down off the pizza shop's steps. One of the white boys, a well-built kid, maybe 18 or 19, with a wavy black pompadour cascading into his large eyes, put on a show of charging the Impala.

"Niggers, get the fu..."

Suddenly, the Impala jerked and then stalled. Before the charging white boy was able to complete his curse, he realized, to his horror, that the car had stopped and that he was within inches of Chance's door.

The rampaging white boy caught his balance before he crashed into the car. Chance could see the terror in his large eyes.

For a long moment everyone froze. The boys in the car. The boys in front of Mama Rosa's. The men on the church steps. The kids who had been playing tag and, the old ladies under their shawls.

Then out of the corner of his eye, Chance caught a blur of motion as X bolted across him and exploded out the car's door.

The white boy, who had been knocked to the brick pavement by the opening door, stared in horror, first at the yellow hand, wrapped up to its wrist with his T-shirt that had been pulled up tight around his neck, and then at the blue-gray barrel of a pistol that had come out of nowhere, but was now pressed to the tip of his bleeding nose.

"I don't think I caught what you said. So why don't you repeat it?" The words, carefully formed, slid slowly from X's lips, which had parted in a thin smile.

X dropped to one knee and brought his cold, flat, gray eyes close to the white boy's crimson flushed face.

The face was familiar to X. This white boy, with his straight nose, strong jaw and deep set eyes, had a face he had seen a thousand times before. X knew this face, if not the boy, and what he knew best were the eyes. These eyes, understandably less cocky now, had haunted his dreams and filled him with questions, and now here they were again, except he wasn't dreaming and the eyes had come to him this time on his terms. X smiled again as he considered the reassuring weight resting cold and hard in his left hand.

Chance was the next person on the street to move and he found himself clutching X around his waist, struggling to pull him up off the limp and terrified white boy.

"Get the car started," yelled O.D.

Roach instantly sobered as he also locked his arms around X as he and Chance crawled back toward the car.

Biggie twisted and twisted at the ignition key. O.D. mimicked Biggie, pounding on an imaginary steering wheel and pumping at a gas pedal that existed only in his mind.

Chance didn't remember getting into the car. All he knew was that he was moving, and not under his own power, and that the shouting voices that had seemed to be all over him just seconds ago were fading in the distance.

"Close the damn door before your ass falls out," shouted Biggie, releasing his grip at the back of Chance's shirt.

Still in a fog, Chance didn't respond. Roach had to lean over him from the back seat in order to grab the handle and pull the door shut.

O.D., his heart banging in his ears, swiveled his head on its massive neck to scan the street for the flashing red and blue lights of police cars.

"Man, we betta get off Euclid and slide on down one of these side streets," warned O.D. in a voice that was raised to a falsetto.

Biggie gunned the engine again, sending the Impala fish-tailing before he was able to regain control.

"Damn, man slow down before you kill us," Roach complained, as he assisted O.D. with his surveillance.

The Impala leapt left, darting in front of oncoming traffic, and then down a street that had been dangerously narrowed by the cars parked on either side.

X pressed his knees hard to the back of his wrists. His hands hung limply between his legs still fused to the butt of the .22. Despite the pressure he concentrated in his knees, X was unable to control the tremors that convulsed his body.

All X could think about was stopping the shaking. He pressed the back of his head hard against the top of the car seat and sucked greedily at the air crashing through the windows. His nostrils flared so wide that his top lip ached from the strain. The night air was so cold that it burned the inside of his head and the heat pooled behind his shut eyes.

The air rushing through the window gave X the sensation that his head was being torn from his body. The decapitation, freed him from his trembling body, and X found the calm he had been searching for. His eyes sunk deeper into their dry sockets as his nosed continued to vacuum the night air.

The hint of a smile that turned up in the corners of X's now placid face was the first image Chance's eyes were able to focus on since being pulled back into the car. Slowly, fragments of memory, like the colorful flakes in a kaleidoscope, fluttered in Chance's minds, twisting and turning until they locked into position and brought him back to awareness.

It was when the last bright, shard of color found its place that Chance was struck by how out of place X's calm, smiling face was.

"Shit man, you must be crazy. What the fuck were you doing?" The words exploded from Chance's mouth and hit X like a slap, but X didn't flinch, but remained peaceful and smiling.

"Give me that damn gun, stupid sonofabitch," exhaled Chance in disgust as he reached for the .22.

Cupping the top of X's hands, Chance tugged at his friend's right knee trying to free the gun.

Looking over at X's upturned face, Chance couldn't understand how his face could appear so relaxed while he exerted such tension on his knees. It made no sense, but then nothing had made much sense these past few days, these past few months.

"Be careful that it don't go off in here," said Biggie, glancing over at the action at his side and then quickly back to the road.

"Drive down to the lake," ordered Chance, now cuddling the gun in his lap.

"To the lake for what?" asked O.D., still scanning the horizon.

"We got to get rid of the gun before we get stopped by the cops."

The mention of police hit O.D. like a fist in the stomach and he doubled over burying his face in his hands.

"Hell, toss that shit out the window right now," shouted Biggie, now even more concerned about the cops.

"Just drive to the damn lake. You think you can handle that?" Anger rose in Chance's voice.

"Whatcha going to do? Shoot me?" Biggie responded.

"Man, Biggie, just shut up and drive," said Roach, clamping a hand on Biggie's shoulders. "Just drive and be cool."

The Impala's wheels spat gravel as the car turned into the stone-covered lot of Lakefront Park. The car's lights bounced off three parked cars, the cars' occupants hidden by the steam that coated the windows.

"Go to the end of the lot and turn off the lights," whispered Chance.

Biggie complied.

"O.D., you come with me," Chance ordered.

"What? Why I got to go?" O.D. wanted to know.

"I need someone to keep a watch down by the water to make sure ain't nobody scoping us," explained Chance, quickly becoming exasperated with O.D.

"Like I said, why me? I ain't the only person in this car with eyes," O.D. half whined.

"Damn. I'll go," said Roach, already easing his skinny frame out the back door.

Chance and Roach walked briskly toward the collection of large boulders and mammoth slabs of concrete that were tied together by a rusted tangle of steel beams, rods, and cable.

The two boys felt their way slowly up the craggy mass and then moved out toward the sounds of the waves slapping at the man-made structure.

Reaching the water's edge, the boys twisted on the balls of their feet, searching for a secure foothold. Chance took one more cursory look around him to make sure that they weren't being watched. It was a precaution that was totally unnecessary since he could barely see Roach, who was just two arm lengths away.

The gun splashed heavily out into the blackness. Two hollow slaps against the water immediately followed the gun's splash. Chance looked over in Roach's direction.

"Pick up a couple of rocks and throw them in. If anybody is watching, they will think we are just skipping stones," Roach said in explanation.

Chance bent over, fingered a stone, and then hoisted it out into the darkness. The boys retraced their steps as best they could back to the car.

"What took y'all so long. I don't like just sitting here like this," said O.D.

"My grandmother don't live far from here. I think I'm going to take the car over to her house and park it in her garage. I don't want to be driving round no more than I have to," announced Biggie.

"Then what?" asked Roach.

"Then I'm going to spend the night. I doubt if anyone is goin to be looking for us in the morning."

"What about us?" O.D. whined.

"Y'all can stay at my grandma's or you can catch the bus home. But I ain't driving no where else tonight."

"Cool then, we be walking," said Roach, speaking for Chance, who was already stepping from the car.

"I'm going with Biggie. Ain't no telling how far you have to walk before a bus come along," said O.D.

"X?" Chance looked at the boy in the sweatshirt, his head still tilted back on the seat, his eyes fixed on the car's roof.

"I think I will stroll with you brothers."

The three boys walked in silence. They didn't acknowledge Biggie when he tapped the horn as he drove by. They watched as the red tail lights dimmed into tiny dots and then evaporated.

"I wasn't really going to shoot nobody," said X, finally fed up with the question the silence had repeated for the last eight blocks.

The only response was the sound of footsteps as the boys kept their steady pace.

"I wasn't going to shoot," X said again, trying to convince himself as much as he was his friends.

The silence wasn't broken again for 20 minutes when the bus pulled to a stop, yellow lights flashing, breaks squeaking. The tall doors yawned open with a deep moan.

X fingered the grab bar and pulled himself onto the bus' rubber steps. Chance followed, but looked back when he counted out coins into the coin box.

"You need some money? Don't worry I gottcha covered," said Chance, looking out at Roach who stood motionless on the sidewalk.

"Naw, thanks. I think I'll catch the next bus." Roach gave a little salute and stepped back from the bus stop.

Before Chance could ask Roach where he was going, the doors wheezed shut and the bus rumbled away.

CHAPTER 13

THE BED VIBRATED IN QUICK, SHORT LEFT AND RIGHT JERKS that made Chance feel like he was laying in a prospector's pan, being shaken to separate worthless silt and gravel from the precious flakes of gold.

There was certainly nothing golden about this night, Chance thought to himself as the Magic Fingers did their thing. The observation spread a wry half smile across his face.

A metallic click came from just above Chance's head, which rested on a pillow that was barely visible under his massive Afro. The bed stopped in mid-spasm. The tiny hum of an electric motor evaporated into silence.

Chance raised up slightly, just enough to reach out and finger a stack of quarters that stood on the combination night stand and floor lamp next to the bed. His fingers toppled the tower of ten quarters, which had originally numbered fifteen. The silver coins spilled out noisily across the night stand's brown Formica top, which had been marked with raised cigarette burn welts. Two of the quarters rolled off the night stand and dropped into the puke green shag carpet that lined the tiny room from wall to wall.

The tips of Chance's fingers traced blindly across the surface of the nightstand until they bumped into one of the quarters. Plucking the coin up he sat up in the bed and slipped the quarter into the silver box attached to the side of the headboard. The Magic Fingers whirred back into action for another four minutes and 38 seconds, not the 'Five-minutes of pure bliss'" promised in all capital letters on the gold-tone sticker stuck on the front of the coin box.

Chance had discovered the false advertising claim after timing the first $1.25 worth of massages.

But just for good measure he decided to time the mechanical fingers again and held the Timex strapped to his wrist about eight inches above the bridge of his nose.

When the sixth, less than blissful ride on the quivering springs came to a jerky halt, again four minutes and 38 seconds long, Chance simply lay still.

Laying still was exactly what he hadn't wanted to do. He knew there was no way to stop from rewinding the film in his head and be forced to go through the events of earlier that evening frame by frame for at least the hundredth time.

"Damn, damn, damn," Chance shouted at the ceiling as he rolled over and tossed his scrawny legs over the side of the bed, his silk socks bringing sparks as they brushed across the shag rug.

Bent over, his chin resting on his chest, Chance kneaded the back of his neck with his hands and thought again of the spray of wine that had placed him in his present sorry situation.

He wasn't supposed to be sitting in the El Dorado motel, in the dark, by himself. Not on this night..

He was supposed to be writhing in the heat of passion right now, Jackie's thick saffron-colored legs wrapped in a tight searing knot around his sweating back.

Smokey Robinson was supposed to be crooning - I love you baby, love you baby, love you from the bottom of my heart. And, what love, has joined, together, don't let nobody take it apart ....from the portable 8-track that sat mute on top of the television.

The motel room was supposed to be bathed in the soft light of the candles he had carefully lined up on a sheet of tin foil on the dresser. And, the heavy aroma of jasmine incense should have been wafting through the room topping off the romantic mood he had planned so meticulously.

Chance pounded a fist into the palm of his left hand, stood up and walked into the bathroom for the tenth time in the last hour.

The bathroom's florescent light buzzed on. It flickered bright then dimmed and then pulsed bright again. The throb of illumination sent a roach scurrying across the sink, up the water stained wall and under the bottom edge of the mirrored medicine cabinet.

Chance twisted on the faucet and brought two palms of cold water to his chin and then buried his face into the icy liquid. Pulling his face from his hands he took a deep breath, blinked rapidly to knock the water from his eyes, wiped his face dry with a towel and headed back into the room.

On his way back to the bed he grabbed one of the two bottles of Cold Duck champagne that sat chilling in a plastic wastebasket half filled with ice.

Pulling the silver foil from the top of the wine bottle, Chance slowly untwisted the wire mesh covering the plastic cork. He pushed up the stopper with his thumbs. The cork popped from the bottle's green neck, hit the ceiling and ricocheted to the rug. A foam of wine seeped over the lip of the bottle and down its sides.

"Why couldn't I do that two hours ago?" Chance cursed at himself as he turned the wine up to his lips.

Two hours ago when he had uncorked a bottle of Cold Duck there had been an explosion that sent a stream of wine spraying in every direction. Before the champagne shower subsided, the bottle was half empty.

Chance took three long pulls on the bottle. He replayed the scene once more in his mind.

Reaching out, Chance grabbed the phone and twisted out seven numbers. The phone rang three times.

"It's your dime," came the voice at the other end of the line.

"This is Chance, whatcha you up to ?"

"Damn, I should be asking you that question. Ain't you the brother who's out on a prom date with Jackie Ealey?"

"It's a long story."

"I gots time and it seems you do too." X laughed into the receiver.

Chance started slowly with the explanation, but X, with some prodding, was eventually successful in getting him to skip over most of the details to get to the point.

"So you telling me that when you opened the champagne it sprayed all over Jackie? Damn, that's some funny shit."

"Yeah, I thought so too man. As a matter of fact I started laughing and couldn't stop."

"That shit must of pissed her off something terrible," observed X.

"I mean you sitting there laughing and she dripping wet and shit. I thought I done raised you better than that boy."

"Fuck you X," snapped Chance, no real anger in his voice.

"So, what happened when you finally stopped laughing?"

"Well, Jackie's crying and cussing right, and at the same time talking 'bout I ruined her dress and hair and that she wants me to take her home."

"Yeah, so?"

"So I take her home. Of course, I'm apologizing all the way and trying to explain that I wasn't laughing at her but at myself. You know, trying to explain that I was trying to be all cool and dapper and all and then bungled everything."

"She didn't buy none of that shit, did she?"

"Well, I thought she understood 'cause she had stopped crying and had stopped cussing me out by the time we pulled up in her drive. Anyway, I waited for her in the car, must have been about twenty minutes and she never did come back out."

"You expected her to come back out?"

"Like I said, I thought she had mellowed out."

"Fool, why did you even take her home? I mean you were in the motel room. You should have just have given her your robe."

"I never made it to the room. This shit all happened in the parking lot outside the prom. You know, I figured I'd start setting the mood before we got to the room and all."

"Yeah, you set the mood alright, mothafucka," X howled into the receiver.

Chance could envision his friend doubled over in spasms of laughter.

After regaining his composure, X coaxed Chance into telling him the story again but with the details he had wanted to skip before.

"So what's up?" X asked at the conclusion of the second telling of the tale.

"I figure there ain't no need for the room to go to waste and shit. Hell, I already done shelled out $18. Why don't you slide by and get O.D. and then pick up some ribs at Whitmore's. I got a couple bottles of champagne left. Hell, we can play some bid whist and shit."

"Sounds good, my man. Should I try to round up Roach and Biggie?"

"I'll call Bigs, if I can find him, but don't go digging up the damn junkie Roach."

"Damn, that's cold," protested X. "Roach is just going through some changes and he needs somebody to help him out. He needs his boys to stand by him."

"You stand by him if you want, but I don't want to be bothered with his sorry ass. The fool gets on my last nerve."

"That's cold."

"That's the way it is," snapped Chance.

"Hey brotha, my name is Wes and I ain't in this mess. That's between you and Roach. I'll see you in 30 ticks."

"Cool, I'll be here, I ain't got no place to go." With that Chance placed the receiver in its cradle and took another long pull on the bottle.

Chance again thought about calling Cheryl. He had dialed her number twice already that evening but had hung up before getting an answer. He wanted to talk to her, but he just didn't know what he wanted to say. He had practiced several apologies out loud while sitting alone in the room, but none of them seemed sincere enough. He had no qualms about begging for her forgiveness. The problem was that he couldn't think of a lie convincing enough to explain why he had taken Jackie to the prom and not her. After all, he had been dating Cheryl for over a year now.

Laying on the bed staring at the ceiling, Chance again attempted to compose an apology. Maybe Cheryl would see the irony in the fact that he was sitting all alone in a motel room and would forgive him, figuring that through the cosmic justice of what goes around comes around, that he had already been punished for his betrayal. Maybe if she thought that, she would decide to no longer be angry with him and would come to the motel, if not to soothe his bruised ego, at least to gloat.

Just having Cheryl near him, even if she took the opportunity to assume the superior moral position, was all he wanted. He just wanted to hear her voice, even if her words weren't endearing.

Chance knew he was grasping at faint hopes, but he didn't want to give in to the possibility that maybe their relationship was beyond repair.

Damn he really wanted to talk to her.

That is what Chance liked most about Cheryl. He had always been able to confide in her and be himself with her without feeling self conscious. He didn't have to wear a macho mask with Cheryl. She allowed him to give voice to his dreams, his fears, and his confusions. Sometimes she would offer sound advice or provide clear insight and make him consider points that he hadn't even thought about. Sometimes she would just listen in silence, opening herself to catch the emotions he poured into her.

Many times he and Cheryl would sit on her front porch and talk for hours and still have a lot more to say to each other by the time her mother flicked the porch light on and off signaling that it was time for him to go.

Chance particularly liked sitting on the porch with his head between Cheryl's nutmeg legs. He would be on the top step and Cheryl would be seated slightly above and behind him on the worn wooden slats of the porch, a firm slender thigh at either side of his face. Chance would lean back, eyes closed, head resting against her belly as her slender fingers twisted his hair into tight braids that would make his scalp tingle with pleasure. Sitting between Cheryl's legs, feeling her warmth, smelling her aroma, talking while having his hair braided was as good as sex, and with Cheryl even better, since that was something they hadn't done. For months they had played around the edges of sex, feeling and squeezing one another to near ecstasy. Yet they had always stopped short of actually doing it. She out of fear of getting pregnant. He out of fear of falling in love.

Chance was afraid of love, of being too close. He had been burned by love, at least what he had thought was love and vowed it would never happen again. Although he had only been in the ninth grade at the time, he felt he had been in love with Leslie Luster. He had opened up to her, spent his allowance on her freely, taking her to movies, to Golden Point for burgers and fries at least twice a week, to the movies at the Shaker Theater, and to the basketball games she half dragged him to because she "loves" the game.

For two months he lavished his attention and his little piece of money on Leslie until he had finally gotten up the nerve to tell her how he felt, how he wanted her to be his lady.

Leslie had listened intently, smiling warmly Chance thought, as he stammered out his intentions. Leslie explained that she just wanted to be friends.

A week after Leslie had demoted him to a "friend" and broken his heart, she was dating Billy Jefferies, a junior and the starting forward on the J.F.K. basketball team. Chance was slow at some things and it took him awhile before he realized, thanks to the not-so-subtle insights of his boys, particularly Biggie. "Fool, you got played. You was taking her to the basketball games so she could watch Billy Jefferies."

Chance had learned his lesson well and had been careful since to guard against forming any emotional attachment. That is why he had been careful to maintain a wall between himself and Cheryl. Anytime he felt that he was getting too close, Chance would focus on some behavioral quirk or some trivial imperfection with Cheryl's body to help bolster his wall.

However, fixating on the fact that she bit her nails when she was nervous, or the fact that she had a rather high forehead, no longer provided strong enough mortar for his wall, and he felt his resistance steadily crumbling over the last few months. He knew that if he had sex with Cheryl, he would fall in love with her and he wasn't willing to take that risk.

On the rare occasion when Chance did have sex, it was always with someone he knew he would never have an emotional attachment. He had determined that what he wanted was a wham-bam-thank-you-ma'am relationship with women. He wanted to remain emotionally detached while physically coupled. He didn't want to talk during sex. He didn't want to whisper sweet nothings into her ear while they were doing it. And after it was over he didn't want to lie around and be placed in a position of carrying on a conversation.

What he wanted was to simply do his do, roll off, roll over and the roll out the door. He had long ago decided that was the perfect relationship.

Sex and the perfect prom night, which wouldn't be perfect unless it ended up in a motel room with him screwing his brains out, is why Chance had asked Jackie to the prom. Although, Chance had no way of knowing for sure that Jackie would give it up. He had reasoned however, that since Jackie had dated both Walter Bankton, the school's star running-back and Levy Banes, who drove a brand new red Cougar, and was known as a player, that she had to be doing something. Certainly, two brothers with the reps of Walter and Levy wouldn't waste time on a broad who wasn't giving up the booty.

Chance had even heard a rumor that Jackie gave blow jobs, but that bit of news came from Teaspoon Phillips, who lied even when he didn't have to just because he liked to lie.

That would really be something if she did, but Chance doubted it, not just because Teaspoon was a liar, but because he had only heard of white girls doing shit that freaky, unless of course a broad was a prostitute.

Still, when Jackie accepted Chance's invitation to go to the prom, he couldn't help but to fantasize over all the possibilities of all they were going to do. Yet, even the daydreams about sex couldn't push the guilt to the back of Chance's mind.

Jackie had asked about Cheryl before she had accepted his invitation and Chance had assured her that he and Cheryl had a falling out and had broken up. It was only half a lie. Cheryl and Chance hadn't broken up, not officially, but they had an argument and hadn't spoken to each other for five days before Chance had approached Jackie.

It had been an argument that he had manufactured just so he would feel justified in asking Jackie to the prom.

Of course, less than a week after Jackie's acceptance Chance and Cheryl had kissed and made up. In the weeks leading up to the prom Chance avoided talking about the subject with Cheryl, but when she asked him to go shopping with her for a prom dress, he felt he had better drop the bomb.

Although he had practiced his speech in the mirror, and thought out just how he would break the news, Chance stumbled and mumbled badly when he looked into Cheryl's eyes. Somehow he made it through a pitiful apology, stating several times that he had been a fool. He explained that he had only asked Jackie after they had argued and that he thought they were broken up for good. And although he proclaimed that he was probably the luckiest dude all because Cheryl had given him another chance and that the last thing in the world he wanted to do was risk losing her again, that he just didn't feel that it was right to break his date with Jackie, particularly since she had already had a dress made for the prom.

At the time Chance had been very pleased with himself and his explanation to Cheryl. Sure she was upset, but she seemed to understand his predicament. At least she never mentioned Jackie and the prom again. And while Cheryl had been a bit cold and a standoffish to him since his explanation, Chance felt that after the prom was over he would be able to smooth it over.

He looked again at the phone and thought about Cheryl. But instead of dialing he dropped another quarter into the magic fingers, shut his eyes and tried to picture himself between Cheryl's legs, his head tilted back, a comb parting his scalp, and her strong fingers weaving his Afro into long braids.

Right then a bang came at the door.

"Stop jacking-off fool and open up the damn door."

"I got your jack off," yelled Chance, rolling off the bed. He padded over to the door and slid the brass chain jiggling it out of its slot.

The first thing through the door was the garlic and smoked hickory smell of barbecue, which was followed closely by X and O.D.

"Where Biggie?" asked O.D. as he scanned the room looking for the lanky yellow boy.

"He said he would be here after he gets off work in about a half hour," Chance explained as he grabbed the greasy brown paper bag from X and headed to the bed.

The trio sat down around the night stand, Chance and X on the bed and O.D. in a rickety high back chair with a worn red-padded vinyl seat that had been mended in several spots with red masking tape. Chance dug into the bag and handed out the three white, grease-stained cardboard boxes.

"The shoulder dinner is yours and the long ribs is mines," said X. He flipped opened the box Chance had handed him. He lifted up a slice of white bread that held in place the wax paper covering the still steaming contents of the box.

"This is O.D.'s chicken. I think you got my ribs," said X nodding at Chance.

O.D., who claimed that he was converting to the Muslim religion because he wasn't praying to "no white Jesus no more," hurriedly scarfed down his half dozen chicken wings with extra sauce. As he fingered the last of his french fries, twirling them along the bottom of the sides of the box to soak up every drop of tangy sauce, O.D. stared at Chance and X.

"Hey, X, let me have a bone," O.D. finally said.

"Go to hell. You supposed to be Muslim now and shit and here you is talking about eating my ribs. Hell, fool, you were carrying on out in the car talking about black folk always eating swine and shit, and here you is begging for my nasty ass pig."

"You know I'm just getting into the Nation. Man, it's hard breaking old habits. And anyway who says I got to convert all at once?" protested O.D. trying to sound and look pitiful, hoping it would help his cause.

"You better pull a bean pie out of your pocket cause you ain't getting nothing here," said X.

"Don't even look over this way," warned Chance not looking up from his food to slap X a greasy-fingered five.

"Well, screw you greedy hoes then. I didn't want that shit no way. Y'all just killing yourself putting that swine in you moufs. Man, pork pickles your brain, makes you dim witted and gives you, what's that shit called? Trick...something or other, you know that worm shit," said OD, his voice rising in agitation.

"But I tell you one thing. This damn swine shonuff is good," said X sucking noisily on a rib bone that he twirled between his shiny lips.

He and Chance busted out in laughter.

Their laughter irritated O.D. almost as much as the growling in his half-empty belly.

"So, Sweetback, where is your lady? I heard she dumped your punk ass after you took her out to dinner and the prom. Played you like a game of checkers," said O.D., hoping his words would dig into Chance.

"Hey, what can I say. I've been played."

"You can say that again you sorry chump," spat O.D., snatching the open bottle of Cold Duck out the wastebasket, sloshing some of the wine on the front his rainbow print polyester shirt.

"Shit. I just bought this shirt and your cheap wine got all over me. Shit, some towels in the bathroom to get this shit off me?" cursed O.D., pulling the wet spot away from his body.

"Damn, I guess that means you ain't going to give me no pussy tonight either," Chance said, laughing.

Try as he might O.D., wanting to be mad, couldn't suppress his laughter either and nearly choked on the wine in his mouth as he padded to the bathroom.

"I tell you one thing, that Cold Duck some kind of unruly tonight," cackled X.

"Stop wiping your shirt and turn on the tube. Make yourself useful," said Chance through a mouthful of shoulder sandwich.

O.D. stomped from the bathroom dabbing a towel to his shirt and turned on the television.

"What's on?" O.D. asked.

"Turn to channel 5. I think Don Kirshner's Rock Concert is on," said X.

The long-haired white boys jumping across the stage on the television sang into mics, tossing their hair back out of their eyes, but it was Al Green's voice that filled the tiny motel room as it blared from the 8-track player on top of the television.

"Who them muthafuckas, Three Dog Night or some shit?" asked X, shuffling and reshuffling a dog-eared deck of cards.

"Who knows?" said Chance.

"Can somebody tell me why we got the tube on with no sound? Why don't we just turn the shit off and listen to the tape player?" O.D. inquired.

"Well, turn off the damn TV then," said X.

But before O.D. could lift his bulk out of the chair, Biggie banged on the door.

"Well, it's bout time," said X.

"Don't waste no time talking. Deal em out. I'm ready to send somebody to Boston tonight and I don't care who it is," said Big, tossing his brown UPS jacket over the television.

"Whatcha got to drink?"

Chance pointed to the wastebasket.

"That's exactly what I thought. That's why I bought this along." Big pulled a pint of 151 Rum from inside his jacket.

"I'm going to the machine and get some Coke," said X.

"Don't bother. I already tried it and it's broke," Big informed his friend.

"Shit, how we going to drink that shit?" O.D. asked, wrinkling his face at the thought of drinking straight rum.

"I don't know about you but I's going to sip mine's right out of this here bottle. Of course if you can't handle that, you can cut it with Cold Duck," said Big taking a long swig of rum. He rolled the warm liquid in his mouth, swishing the liquor against the side of one cheek, then against the other. The rum began to vaporize, burning behind his shut eyes and stinging the interior of his nose. Then he titled back his head, tensed his shoulders and swallowed hard.

"Alright, who's next?" Big asked hoarsely as he held out the Bacardi bottle.

The tiny motel room soon filled with the sounds of a liquor-fueled bid-whist marathon; loud talk, woof-tickets, in-your-face insults, the slap of set cards to foreheads and rib-rattling laughter.

Chance woke with a start. Panic gripped him when he realized that the bed that was jerking wasn't his bed. He tried to focus his eyes and as the blurs of Big slumped in the chair and O.D. stretched across the floor slowly became clear, Chance's anxiety melted away.

"I thought that would wake your dead ass up," said X, who had just deposited the quarter he found on the carpet into the Magic Fingers.

It also became clear to Chance that mixing Cold Duck and rum, as Big had suggested, hadn't been a very good idea.

"Here, put this on the back of your neck," said X tossing Chance a cold wet washcloth that had the last bits of ice from the waste basket twisted inside of it.

"What time is it?" asked Chance, the wet rag sending fingers of cold water trailing down his back.

"Something after four. You fools been sleep about an hour," said X, flinging one card at a time from the deck in his palm at O.D.'s gaping mouth. The snoring teen, spread eagle on the green shag carpet, didn't flinch when a card grazed his chin or bounced off the bridge of his nose.

"That hog-calling fool dead to the world," X said, placing the what remained of the deck on the night stand having tired of target practice.

"You didn't pass out?" asked Chance, sleep still holding onto him stubbornly.

Naw, I didn't drink half as much as y'all. So I've just been sitting here thinking."

" Bout what?"

"I don't know, I guess about all of us and all the shit we've been through over the years. You know I've known you, O.D., Big, and Roach since elementary school. And now here we are all bout to go our separate ways."

Chance sat quiet for awhile trying to shake the cobwebs from his mind as X's words slowly filtered in through the rum fog. Chance didn't want to admit it, but he too knew things were changing. In another three months he would be a freshman at Ohio University.

Chance looked down at the sleeping figure of O.D. and remembered how his friend had talked about going to college too. But it was just talk. What O.D. did best was eat, drink and pass out and they don't give degrees in that. Hell, if the truth be told O.D. would be lucky to graduate with the class, he'd probably have to go to summer school to make up a few classes.

Biggie, who had dropped out of school three months earlier, so he could work full-time, was making good money on the third shift at UPS loading and unloading trucks. He had been talking about marrying his girlfriend Jennifer, who had given birth to his twin girls, Kelly and Kalli, six months earlier.

Biggie's mother about died when he dropped out. She couldn't understand his defiance and still steadfastly refused to accept the fact the she was a grandmother. Biggie used his mother's objection to the baby girls as a way to deflect Jennifer's questions about marriage.

"Jen, just give her sometime to get used to the idea of me being a father first. When she's ready to deal with that, then we can talk bout hooking up." Biggie already knew he didn't feel about Jennifer in that way, and although he enjoyed playing with his baby girls, the real joy he got from them was that their existence was maddening for his mother.

And then there was Roach. Looking more like Jimi Hendrix than Jim Hendrix. More than six months ago Roach had all but dropped out of sight and started shacking with some white hippy, college girl and six other acid-tripping white freaks. The white kids were all college kids at Case Western and they shared a house that they had painted in psychedelic colors down off Coventry, which was Cleveland's version of San Francisco's Haight-Asbury.

A year earlier, because he was getting high so much, Roach's parents had taken him out of Kennedy and had enrolled him in Cathedral Latin, an all boys Catholic school. They thought a change in environment would turn Roach around. His parents didn't see the connection between their constant drinking and Roach's pill popping.

Changing schools had only made matters worse. He started hanging with the well-to-do white boys at Latin, who gave him unlimited access to drugs. At first Roach would come up to the Mount, when he was still socializing with his "black friends" and describe his acid trips-window pane, orange sunshine, LSD in great detail. But after his stories no longer pulled an audience, he came around less and less often. Then one day, before anyone had really noticed, Roach had all but disappeared from the set.

Roach didn't make any sense to Chance. He had claimed it was because of the freaky white pussy that he hung with, the flower children hippies, but to Chance it seemed that Roach was trying to distance himself from his blackness. Roach claimed he was just in a different groove, a groove that was too heavy for his old friends to understand. Chance wondered if drugs provided Roach with the same sense of peace he had once told Chance he found on his one man treks to the Cuyahoga River.

"You know I'm proud of you, boy," said X, pulling Chance from his thoughts. "You going to college and shit and you going to do exactly what you always said you wanted to do, be a writer and shit. You better acknowledge my ass in the foreword of your first novel."

The words X spoke had caught Chance off guard. It was very seldom that any of them expressed themselves, let alone complimented one another.

Chance felt a little ashamed. He was always talking about what he wanted do, yet he hadn't really pressed them to open up, and he realized at that moment how little he really knew about X or any of his boys.

Months earlier Chance had been surprised that they all weren't going to college. And even though Biggie had dropped out, he figured he would get his GED, maybe go to community college for a couple years and then finish his degree at a four-year school. Chance just assumed that's what everybody did after graduating from high school.

He had always known he was going to college. So it was strange to realize that he was the only one going.

"So, X, what you going to do? I mean, I ain't heard you talk about going to school or nothing. I mean what is it you want to do with your life?" said Chance.

"You know, that's the first time you ever asked me about my life." X immediately saw the pained looked that stole across Chance's face.

"Now don't go acting like I'm putting you down. Ain't none of us really dug deeper than the surface. Hell, I ain't never asked you about wanting to be a writer. Of course, you always talking about what you was going to do, so nobody had to ask. But I don't know if I would have asked you if you hadn't have given up the information."

"Why do you think that is?" asked Chance.

X didn't answer.

"I've been thinking about joining the Marines. You know my old man was a Marine," said X.

"Who, Mr. Johnson?" Chance couldn't picture old man Johnson, with his bum leg being in the Marines. But, maybe he had got his leg injured in the war. Funny how we never see old people as ever being young, Chance thought to himself.

"Naw, I'm talking about my real father. My mom got a picture of him in his uniform. She got it hid with some of his letters in the lining of an old coat she got in a cedar chest in the attic. She don't know I know about him," continued X.

"Why do you think she never told you?"

"Probably because she didn't want me to know I'm a bastard," laughed X.

"Man, don't say that." The word bastard had stung Chance deeply and he didn't want to hear his friend talk about himself like that.

"Man, you don't know that. I mean it's just as likely that they were married and they got divorced."

"Naw, they didn't get married."

"How, do you know?" said Chance trying to get X to acknowledge another possibility.

"I just know, alright."

Silence filled the room again. Chance didn't know if he should wait for X to continue his story. This was new territory talking about something personal, sharing intimate secrets. The silence stretched for a what seemed like a very long while before Chance ventured on.

"So what else you know about him, your father? I mean, have you ever talked to him?"

"Naw, ain't nothing happenin' like that. I don't even know if the dude know anything about me. I don't think my Moms knows that I know. I'll talk to you about it one day when the time's right."

"When's that?"

"I can't say exactly when, but I'll know when the time's right," continued X, his voice sounding tired.

"I guess you wondering why I'm telling you this shit now?" he continued," I guess it's because I got this feeling that we all going in different directions and, hell, this maybe the last time I see you."

"Man whatcha talking about? We always going to be tight, I mean we like family. Going back to the third grade and shit." Somehow X's statement had frightened Chance.

"Brotha, open up your eyes. We already drifting apart. I guess that's why it hurt me when you dogged Roach like you did. Talking about you didn't want to be around his junkie ass. It just made me realize how puny these bonds of friendship between us really are."

Chance was ashamed and even a little angry. Still, he knew what X was saying was right. As close as they all had been, nearly everyday for the last dozen years, playing, roughhousing, fighting, chasing girls, partying, they had never really opened up to one another. Perhaps that was something that dudes just didn't do because they were too busy living life to be sitting around analyzing it.

It was strange to Chance that he had never detected that oversight before, but now it yawned before him like a great chasm. He now was aware of this void between him and his friends, particularly X, and felt disheartened by the knowledge that the void would probably always remain.

"So why did you lay this all on me and why now?" For some reason, that didn't make sense to Chance, he was feeling himself becoming angry.

"I don't really know. At least about why I'm spilling my guts now. I never had the urge to tell anyone about my father before. I just don't know? Like I said, maybe it's the fact that we are going our separate ways. Going to different lives to become different people," X paused for a second and then continued.

"I told you because you are the smart one."

Chance shaking his head started to protest.

"Yes, you are. Who knows maybe instead of becoming a writer you might decide to become a shrink and if that's the case, maybe you can make some sense out of my life." X smiled hoping that Chance understood that he was joking.

"I'm sure you will do that long before I'm out of school," said Chance.

"Damn, I sure hope so, because the shit sure is crazy now," X quipped.

"The thing to remember is that everybody is screwed up in their own way."

"Was that shit supposed to be heavy or something?"

"What, you didn't think that was deep?" Chance asked.

"Hell, I'll give you deep. I'll get deep in your ass on the b-ball court right now," said X, his trademark impish grin lighting his face again. X had wanted to say more about his father and how he was feeling, but he didn't know how, so he simply switched gears.

"What? Right now?" Chance looked at his watch.

"You must be out of your mind. It's only 4:30 in the morning. Man, it's pitch black outside."

"So. We'll go up to the Mount and play under the car lights. Hell, I'm going to bust your eyes out with my first couple shots anyway," said X as he leaped in the air, his Afro scrapping the ceiling, and arched an imaginary ball through an imaginary net. "Boom. Just like that. All net."

"Well, let's get it on," said Chance heading to the door. At the door he paused and looked back into the room at O.D. and Big, both snoring like champion hog callers.

"We can bring em back some breakfast after I finish kicking your ass," said X, as he walked by Chance and jogged to the car.

Chance felt for the room key in his pockets. Finding it, he hit the wall switch, killing the light and then pulled the door shut.

Million Man March
1995

CHAPTER 14

THE SKITTISH WHITE MAN, HIS GRAYING BLOND HAIR sticking up all over his head, several loose strands pasted down across his forehead and touching the lid of his left eye, picked his way carefully through the river of black men.

Pushed along in the current of dark males, he moved briskly through the wide streets overflowing with black men. Bobbing along in the human flow, he concentrated only on his position, keenly aware not to lose contact with his black man.

"How do you want to work this?" the white man asked, twisting his body and redirecting it to his left, fighting not to be pushed into the flow of the human tributary surging to the right and away from Chance.

He pressed a hand to his wild mane of hair and broke into a quick step, jostling his way through the crush of bodies and nearly bumping into Chance as he came up on the black reporter's right shoulder. He had to short hop in order not to do exactly that.

"Do you think we should stay together and work the crowd?"

The white man's words sounded more like a plea than a question. Chance didn't turn to acknowledge the man's presence, deciding instead to make his colleague sweat a little. Maintaining his forward gaze, Chance waited more than a minute before responding, feeling only the slightest bit of guilt as he relished in the white man's discomfort.

"I don't know, Fergie. I think we probably would do better by splitting up and working the mall separately," Chance finally said, glancing to his left in time to catch the flash of surprise and dismay in the blue-green eyes at his shoulder.

It wasn't the answer the white reporter had wanted to hear, but Fergie wasn't about to admit his concern, although he reasoned to himself that it was quite understandable for someone in his peculiar predicament to be somewhat nervous.

As he dogged Chance's heels, Fergie considered his situation again; a white man in the midst of a million black men. Black men, who he knew would surely enjoy nothing more than releasing their frustrations, probably some of them very legitimate although not of his making, by kicking any white man's ass, which at this moment meant his ass.

As the momentum of the crowd moved him forward, Fergie fingered the tiny silver beaded chain attached to the plastic ID that dangled around his neck like a rosary. Fergie's placid face, hair combed in place, smiled out confidentially from the press credentials that identified him as William Ferguson, Washington Bureau, Cleveland Beacon Herald. The cool silver metal beads slid back and forth between his pink fingers as Fergie scanned the scene in front of him and watched in awe the rivers of black faces, coming from all directions: flowing down the embankment from the Capitol, surging up from the Lincoln Memorial, flooding in from the area around the Smithsonian Museums and emptying out in a dusky confluence onto the National Mall.

Dark faces surrounded him, faces that he realized at that moment did all look alike. He felt something akin to panic rising in him as he turned to look for Chance. For a second he was sure he had lost him and would be hopeless adrift in this ocean of darkness. Just then he regained his bearings, pushed through the three men that separated him from Chance and nuzzled up close behind him. Fergie silently scolded himself for not being more careful, he couldn't afford to let his thoughts drift off, let his attention lapse not even for a few seconds. Otherwise he would most certainly would be separated from his human life preserver in this sea of nig...

Fergie caught himself instantly. He didn't know why that word had crept into his head. He wasn't that type of person, he wasn't prejudiced, it had to be the situation, that was it. The strain of it, surrounded as he was by all these "African-American" men, he repeated the words in his mind "African-American.." A second wave of panic came over him when he wondered had he just thought the "N" word, or had he actually uttered the word.

Fergie sucked in a deep breath, a hint of a wry smile in the corners of his mouth, and he admonished himself for being so irrational. When he felt a hand on his shoulder the wisp of a smile vanished.

"Fergie. Fergie, man."

It took veteran reporter Bill Fergerson, a man with nearly 22 years of award-winning experience, a man who covered the Gulf war, been in Bosnia on two assignments, and who had worked the streets of South Central LA in the wake of the riots sparked by the Rodney King verdict, several excruciating seconds to connect the voice that went with the black hand on his shoulder to his journalistic partner.

"Chance? Chance." Fergie repeated the mantra, "Chance. Chance," as the solid feel of recognition settled in. Fergie fumbled with the narrow reporters pad in his left hand. Flipping it open he freed the pen held in the pad's wire spirals and began scribbling notes, hoping that doing some familiar motor skill would ease his nervousness and help him resume his professional persona.

"Man, this is some crowd. Can you believe the turnout? They expected a million. You think there is a million here?" Fergie realized he was babbling and made a great effort to calm himself.

Feeling an ever increasing sense of guilt in the joy he was taking in Fergie's obvious discomfort, Chance decided to be benevolent. After all, Fergie was alright. As a matter of fact he liked working with the man and always found the white guy's dry, off-beat, sense of humor refreshing.

"Fergie, why don't you take the two-way radio and hook up with the photographer and you two work the march together," said Chance, unclipping the radio from the waistband of his linen slacks. He handed the palm-sized black box of electronics to Fergie.

"What about you? What about art for the folks you interview?"

"I'm going to do something a little different. Take off on my overall impressions of the day. It won't be anything tied to anything, or anyone specific that way the desk can just pull generic wire art of the march to run with my story."

Fergie nodded his acknowledgment, relieved that he wouldn't be alone and would be working with another white face. He had failed to recognize the lifeline Chance had just thrown to him.

Feeling more at ease, Fergie asked, "so where did the photographer say she was going to meet us?" He clipped the radio to his belt, the security of the two-way device tethering him to the world he knew.

"Somewhere near the front steps of the Rayburn Building," said Chance, angling his head toward the U.S. Senate office building a good half-mile away. Both he and Fergie looked at the waves of black men, specks of color, with flags and banners, undecipherable at this distant, moving down the hill in the direction of the Capitol. Chance was filled with pride and his spirit was lifted by the sight.

Fergie swallowed hard as he thought about wading through that dark sea to get to the rendezvous point with the Associated Press photographer.

"Well, okay then. See you back at the bureau when this is all over," said Fergie. He extended a hand in Chance's direction.

Grabbing the white man's hand, Chance pressed it into his firmly, placing his other hand on top, sandwiching Fergie's hand between his.

"Alright, Fergie, meet you back at the ole plantation."

Fergie hesitated, not sure how to react. Was the comment meant as a joke, or was it a slap at him? Then he felt a reassuring squeeze on his hand. Chance squeezed one more time before letting go. Fergie returned Chance's smile, took three steps before being completely swallowed by the black crowd.

Chance reached for his reporter's notebook in his back pocket and did a slow 360 degree turn absorbing the energy of the crowd, waiting for something to catch his eye. Fixing on a small knot of men climbing up the statue some 200 yards away, Chance slowly edged in that direction, writing as he moved.

"Excuse me, brother."

Chance turned in the direction of the rather solid bump at his back, coming as it did from 6 foot 3 or four, 250 pound plus young man who stared down at him, his bald head shining as much in the light of the sun as did the two gold hoops attached to both his ears. He looked like a black Mr. Clean.

"Huh? Ah, no problem," said Chance, knocked off balance as much by the young man's bulk as by his politeness.

"Wallace Reynolds, Long Beach, Calli," said the young man as he extended a beefy hand.

"Chance Marshall, Cleveland." Chance caught the huge paw shoved in his direction and grasped it firmly.

"Man, this is some kind of beautiful, ain't it? I didn't know what I expected. But I sure didn't expect nothin' like this here," a satisfied smile, like you get after popping the last moist piece of cornbread in your mouth after finishing a good down home meal, spread across the young brother's face.

Chance realized that he was still holding the young man's hand, but for some reason he didn't feel awkward, which he did find strange. So much physical intimacy with another man was not normal for him. Chance started to go into his reporter mode, which was very normal and natural for him, and ask the young man exactly what he had expected from the march, but somehow that felt awkward. With no time to ponder what he was feeling, Chance simply placed his other hand over the hand still clinching the hand of the young man.

"Beautiful is the right word. You be cool," Chance said finally and squeezed the young man's hand again before letting it slip away. He watched as the young man moved less than five feet away and then briskly shake another hand.

Chance stood still and just let the crowd surge pass. He was bumped several times but every bump was followed by the words "excuse me." He reached for his reporters pad and scratched his observations.

"Politeness. A sea of politeness. ...Black men from all corners of this country. Black men of all ages, and backgrounds. Frat brothers, gang bangers, clergy, businessmen, fathers, sons, brothers, grandfathers, ..A world of black men. Harmonious congregation."

"You a reporter?"

"Yeah," said Chance lifting his Bic from his pad and flipping the note book shut.

"Oh no, don't go putting that pen up now. I want you to interview me. I got some things I want to say about this here Million Man March. I mean, that's if you think your readers want to hear what an old country boy from Tennessee got on his mind?"

Chance laughed and thumbed up a clean page.

"So, what does this backwoods brother have on his mind?"

"Whoa, hold on back it up. Back it up. There is a big difference between being backwoods and country," a smile simultaneously sparked in the man's dark brown eyes and on his equally dark face.

"Let's begin at the beginning and do it official. Now, what's your name, sir, and where are you from?"

"Samuel James Mercer. Leewood, Tennessee. I goes by S.J. back home."

"Well, S.J., I'm Chance Marshall and I'm a columnist for the Cleveland Beacon Herald." Chance shifted his pen to his left hand and the two men shook hands.

"First, let me go on the record and say that this black man is here because of Brother Farrakhan. You can't separate the messenger from the message, and like the man or not, there wouldn't have been no Million Man March if it wasn't for him. And you can quote me on that," proclaimed S.J., craning his neck slightly to see if Chance was writing down what he said.

"Hey, don't be wasting no ink on S.J. Everybody in Leewood knows that Mrs. Mercer's only boy ain't got the sense he was born with," interrupted a tall, distinguished older gentleman who moved in behind S.J. The tall man, with a camera dangling from his neck sported an amazingly white, thick beard that jumped from his face that was the deep rich color of black olives. The bearded man clamped two large hands on S.J.'s rounded shoulders.

"Mr. Marshall, this rude dude, who just got all up in our conversation is

Purnell Dawes. And up until just a few moments ago we had been friends for 55 years, since we was boys. You think after spending all that time in my company that some of my intelligence would have rubbed off on the man. But, as you can tell, it hasn't." S.J. smiled through a set of yellow teeth that were spaced like pickets in a fence in the man's expansive mouth.

"Did you two travel to Washington together?" asked Chance realizing that he would have to be quick if he was going to wedge a few words of his own between these two.

"Me and him and about thirty others came up from Cobb County, Tennessee by bus. Left Sunday morning 'round four and pulled into the Chocolate City a little after 6:30 this morning."

Purnell took up his friends story before S.J. had shut his mouth good.

"We rode for 26 long hours on that Grey dog with only three rest stops. And let me tell you something, young blood, I'm one colored man who hates traveling by bus so you know I didn't ride all that way with a bunch of hard legs just to see some fool in a bow tie," Purnell squeezed S.J. shoulders and shot Chance a wink his friend couldn't see.

"See, that's your problem Purnell, you always one to parrot what some backwoods Baptist preacher got to say. I don't see that Reverend Brown of yours doing nothing for the black man."

Chance jumped in hoping to head off a debate he was sure these two had had several times before and that he didn't have time to hear.

"So, Mr. Dawes, that's D -A- W- E- S right?" Purnell gave an affirmative nod and Chance continued.

"So exactly why did you come to the march?"

Purnell rolled his tongue against the inside of his cheek as he considered his response. He sucked at his teeth and then answered.

"Frankly, I came to D.C. for me. I came to stand up for me and say to the world, 'I am a man.' I'm a black man who has been taking responsibility for himself, his family and his community. I've been doing it for 63 years and I'm gonna to continue doing exactly that," said Purnell, his words coming slow and measured.

"I came because I wanted to stand here with other black men and affirm our manhood," he continued, lifting his camera to his right eye as he twisted the lens.

"Come on, S.J., smile. Look like you glad to be here," coaxed Purnell.

"Man, get that thing outta my face," protested S.J.

"Come on S.J."

"Look here, Purnell don't be trying to change the subject shooting pictures. Why can't you say you came here to support Farrakhan too?"

"'Cause I didn't." The camera clicked once then whirred as the film advanced.

Now it was S.J.'s turn to focus on Purnell and he fixed a hard stare on his friend.

"You name any one of your black leaders who is willing to speak his mind like the Minister?"

Chance wished he knew shorthand and prayed that he could make sense of his hurried notes when he went back over them later.

"See, you always get worked up when we discuss Farrakhan and I don't know why cuz there ain't nothing you can say that's going to make me feel different bout the man. He's a black bigot and I don't stud no bigots, white or black," said Purnell, refocusing his camera on S.J.

"Man, get that thing out my face," growled SJ, swiping at the camera. "That's exactly your problem, Purnell. You like most black folk, letting the media tell us how to think. They write that he said something about Jews and we fall over ourselves lining up to ah, ah, damn. What's the word? Help me out here."

"Repudiate," Purnell said dryly.

"Yeah, we be all up on the television condemning the brother," said S.J., his voice rising and his words coming out fast and bumping up against one another as he continued his impassioned monologue.

"I'll tell you one thing, and make sure you quote me on this mister reporter," said S.J., snapping his gaze on Chance, tapping an index finger on the reporters note pad. " I'm always going to be 100 percent behind any black man that 100 percent of white America is against."

Finally, there was a pause in the banter between the two old men and Chance quickly took advantage of the lull to extricate himself from the debate.

Flipping shut his notebook, Chance tucked the pen behind his ear. "I just want to thank both of you for talking to me but I got to go out here and get some more quotes."

He left the two men as they continued arguing about Farrakhan.

Wedging his way through the crowd again Chance noticed dozens of tight knots of black men, who just like S.J. and Purnell, appeared to be engulfed in deep conversations, the weight of their discussions underscored by wagging fingers and exaggerated facial gestures.

Chance stopped again, taking several minutes to record the scene around him.

"Yo, Chance. Chance Marshall."

The sound of his name caught him totally off guard. Chance was further unbalanced by the fact he couldn't make out from what direction he was being called.

"Yo, Chance, up here."

Chance looked up at the statue trying to pinpoint who among the three dozen or so men, some wedged in the crock of 10 foot arms, some straddling metal horse flanks and bronze cannon barrels, and still others draped across the statues weathered gray sandstone base their feet dangling 15 feet off the ground.

"Chance, over here." A man, dressed in white African robes, arms outstretched, waved his hands over head.

From this distance it was still hard for Chance to make out any of the distinguishing details that made up the yellow face, framed by a mass of coiled snakes, that was calling out to him. Yet there was definitely something about the dreadlocked man that was familiar, very familiar.

Chance tried to fit together the puzzle pieces as he watched as several pairs of hands carefully lowered the robed man, first to the statue's platform and then into the human shrubbery bunched around the base of the bronze horseman.

When Chance saw the robed figure come toward him in long strides, a confidence in his bolt straight posture and maybe just a touch of arrogance in the tilt of his head, he knew at once who had called his name.

"X? X is that you?" A rush of excitement pushed through Chance as the years that had separated the two men quickly fell away and long ago memories flooded to the surface closing the distant between them quicker than X's elongated steps.

"Damn, man how long has it been? What 15, no 20 years," barked Chance thrusting out his hand.

"What's this handshake shit?" said X in mock rebuke. He slapped Chance's hand aside and enveloped him in the folds of his white robes.

The action had caught Chance off guard. They had never embraced before. Hugging another man wasn't common practice among the black men Chance knew. He didn't even hug his father or brothers and Chance felt awkward in this foreign embrace.

"C'mon give me some love here, brother," blustered X as he pounded at Chance's back with powerful arms that he drew even tighter around his friend.

Chance mentally scrambled to regain his composure and returned the demonstrative greeting, tentatively at first, not quite sure the protocol for hugging another man and still not sure if he even liked this much familiarity.

Chance was relieved when X broke off the embrace to clap his hands to Chance's shoulders. Holding the reporter at arms length, X locked his eyes on his boyhood friend, his long ago ace-boon-coon as they both stood and smiled until their jaws ached.

"Man, I can't believe it's been so long. But you still looking the same, a little less hair, but I knew it was you," said X, releasing his grip and dropping his hands to his sides.

"You too, X, now that I've seen you up close. But I have to tell you those robes and the dreads threw me off.

"It's the new me," said X, turning in a tight circle, his arms outstretched. "And, by the way the name is Mustafa Kahlid Ali."

"Uh, I'm sorry, I didn't mean to, I mean, I didn't know."

X broke in. "Don't go sweating it. Hey, you and me go way too far back for me to be tripping about a name. To you I'm still X, that crazy, wine drinking, chickaboo chasing, dozens playing son of a you know what, who grew up with you on the streets of Lee Harvard." X pulled Chance to him again squeezed him between two pythons masquerading as arms.

This time Chance gave as good as he got.

"So tell me what you've been doing?"

"Everything? Just how much of the last twenty years do you want me to fill in?" asked X.

"Well, let's start with this," said Chance, taking a step back and waving his hands over the white robes.

"Well, about 10 years ago when I was in Saudi."

"Saudi?"

"I'll get to that in a minute. Let me finish this part of the story."

"Sorry."

X continued. "As I was saying, when I was in Saudi, where I was working with an oil company doing materials logistics work, I started talking to this Saudi brother, who managed the operation, about Islam and the more we talked the more I wanted to learn about the religion."

"Ain't you the same brother whose mama 'bout near had a fit when you walked in the house chowing down on a bean pie and carrying a copy of Muhammad Speaks under his arm?"

The image of X's mother waving a wooden spoon over her head with one hand and snapping a dish towel in front of X face with the other as she shooed him and "that damnable devilish Muslim mess" out of her house, brought a grin to Chance's face and water to his eyes.

"Man, she was shonuff some kind of mad. Remember how she swung at me with that wooden spoon and knocked that porcelain sculpture of the Virgin Mary off the fridge. Thing shattered in a million pieces," said X, the laughter rolling from him in spasmatic waves. "The woman went wild, saying it was a sign from God that he had no truck with no black Muslim. Oh, man, my mama was something else again."

"You ain't never lied. You ain't never lied." Chance said nodding agreement.

"Well, anyway, I started studying about eight years ago. Just decided I needed to find something to bring me some peace. And Islam has given me something I could never find with women, drugs, liquor, money or any combination of those four."

"Yeah, that was the last thing I heard about you. I think it was O.D. or Biggie who told me when I came home from school one summer, it might have been my last year at OU, that you were out in L.A., running women and dabbling in a little junk."

"Yeah, I was trying to be like that tired ass Wig. Man, remember how we thought that brother had it going on. Man, we were some knuckleheads back then."

Both men shook their heads at the same time recalling Wig's lectures on life and how it should be lived, lectures that he had delivered between pickup games at the basketball court.

"Anyway, it didn't take me long to realize that I didn't have the game to be a pimp. And it took the two babes I had conned into hustling for me even less time to come to that conclusion. So in less than seven months in the business I found myself a pimp with no employees and even fewer prospects. So I did the straight thing for a while, worked a few odd jobs, started going to UCLA, got married, had two kids, got divorced and then started growing up."

"Dig that. It takes awhile before deciding to become an adult," cosigned Chance.

"Unfortunately some of us never make the transition. That's why something like this is important. A lot of brothers been asleep for too long and it's time they woke up to what is really important," said X. He paused. "You going to want to quote me?" X asked.

Chance felt embarrassed and all he could do was stare nonplussed at X.

"Yeah, Chance, I've been keeping up with you. My moms even sent me a couple of your articles now and then. See you might have forgotten 'bout the homies, but they ain't forgot bout you."

"X, you know it is. When I see your mother I ask 'bout you, but I don't get back to the old neighborhood much." Chance felt even more embarrassed now and realized that he was reaching for his reporter's notebook for a sense of security.

"Hey, nothing to apologize for. That's the way it goes. I mean I haven't been back to Cleveland but maybe half dozen times myself since graduating from Kennedy and I only saw some of the old gang on one visit for Roach's funeral."

"I would have been there but I didn't find out he had died until two months after the funeral. I'm sorry I missed that. Sometimes ..." The thought went no further and evaporated into a deep silence.

"That was one of the articles my mom sent me. The one you wrote about Roach and all of us and how we take people for granted, not appreciating them until they are gone. Man I actually cried when you wrote about going to his grave late at night and having a conversation with him over a box of ribs."

Silence visited them again. They fixed their eyes on the mammoth television screen perched high above the mall on metal scaffolding a few hundred feet away. A young boy in a dashiki, his head crowned by a large Afro, was reading a poem, his grainy giant size image mirrored in another dozen big screens scattered on towering platforms throughout the mall.

However, the young speaker stayed at the edges of Chance's thoughts and quickly gave way to thoughts about Roach.

"It was like I wrote him off after I found out he was hooked on drugs. I mean I spoke with him a few times and fooled myself that I was trying to convince him to get his life together. But both times I called myself having a heart to heart with him, I remember hoping that he wouldn't ask to borrow any money," confessed Chance. "There I was worrying about him hitting me up for a few damn dollars."

"Don't beat yourself up. Roach was a big boy and he knew what he was doing or at least he should have," said X, as he quickly changed the subject.

"So whatcha you hear of O.D. and Biggie?"

"O.D. is doing fine, just fine." Leaning back on his hands Chance repeated what his mother had wrote him about O.D. being a minister of a little church in Kentucky and recently getting married to one of the choir members, a widow with three children all under the age of five.

"Wasn't O.D.'s people from Kentucky or something like that," quizzed X.

"Yeah, I think so. I think a couple of times him and his family went down there on vacation to visit his grandmother and some cousin."

"Now, O.D.'s turning into a preacher ain't no surprise. He fought it for a while, that going to church and all, especially when we got to high school. But before that the boy lived in church. We couldn't even get a good ball game going on Sunday evening until way after 6 'cause O.D. would just be getting in from church. His mama lived at that church, 24-7."

Chance nodded his head in agreement. "Well, I know she is the happiest woman on earth now. Her boy a preacher. It about worried her to death that he was turn out "no account" like his friends."

"Whoa brother, that's hitting close to home," laughed X. "At least she didn't dog us like Biggie's uppity mammy, thinking she was better than everybody in the neighborhood."

Chance took up the story. "Did you ever see the inside of Biggie's crib?"

"Go into the Butler estate? Hell, I was lucky to be allowed to stand and wait in the driveway."

"I thought you being high yellow and shit."

"Don't even go there, Chance."

"You know I'm just messing with you, X. That woman never let any of us set foot inside her house thinking we were a bad influence on her son, all the while he the one talking about try this and let's do this," Chance said.

"My man Biggie was a real piece of work, but he turned out alright. Don't know if his mamma's happy but Bigs doing fine. Saw him about a year ago last Christmas."

"Heard he was working for some computer firm down in Atlanta with a fat wife and couple of kids," chimed in Chance.

"I seen him bout three four years ago round Christmas. And the brother was rotund just like his old lady. Boy had to be tipping the scales at 260, or 270. Biggie living up to his name now." X pushed out his belly and filled his cheeks with air. After holding the ridiculous pose for thirty seconds, X exhaled, his face deflated and the outline of his stomach disappeared as the front of his robe went slack.

"Yeah, saw Bigs and his family when I passed through Atlanta," continued X. Found the brother in the phone book and called from the airport. He came out, picked me up and had me over to his house for dinner. Oh man, we had a good old time laughing and talking about the days." Recalling the dinner brought a warm smile to X's lips.

"What about his twin girls he had with Jennifer?"

She had waited on Biggie for awhile but eventually realized it wasn't only his mother that was keeping them apart. Deciding to get on with her own life, she married.

"Biggie told me the girls are fine. They are both in college. He keeps in touch with them," X continued.

"That's good. Yep, real good." Chance sighed the comment as he thought about his own two kids, a son and a daughter, who for the last six years had been living with his ex-wife in Florida. He saw them every holiday and during the summers and talked to them at least once a week on the phone, but Chance knew it wasn't enough. He had wanted so badly to be the perfect father, giving his kids the love he had always felt his father had withheld from him as a child. Chance wondered if his children knew just how much he loved them.

The two old friends sat down on squares of newspaper that Chance had folded out on the dry, packed dirt of the mall. A half-dozen pair of legs shifted positions to make room for the two men and their newsprint palates. Like buoys tethered in high seas, Chance and X caught up on old times, as shifting waves of legs passed by, their shoulders brushed by the occasional thigh or knee. They both relished the shared history, and savored each memory, drinking the stories in like sips of aged single-malt scotch, swishing around the sepia colored brew of remembrance, lingering over the richness of details coaxed from mental recesses, and finally ingesting the magical mixture, letting its warmth spread throughout them.

Chance looked down at himself and then over at X, both sitting Indian style like they used to do at Cub Scout meetings 30 years earlier. The memory made a smile flash across Chance's face.

"What is it?" The smile had roused X's curiosity.

"Huh? Oh nothing. Just remembering."

"C'mon, brother, give up the details. I ain't seen you in 20 years and you still keeping secrets," said X, readjusting the positions of his legs trying to get comfortable.

Relenting, Chance opened up.

"Remember how the den mothers in Cub Scouts used to make us sit like Indians in a circle and then say grace before we could dive into the cookies and Kool Aid?"

"You mean say grace and repeat the Cub Scout promise," chimed in X, still rearranging his legs. Finally deciding that there was no way to get comfortable, he continued.

"Anyway, the only den mother that made us do that was O.D.'s moms. And the grace was never nothing short and sweet like 'God bless this food. Amen'. Naw, she had to have church up in that kitchen, everybody doing a little sermon. Man, I would have skipped those meetings at O.D.'s if it wasn't for the homemade cookies and cupcakes his mama made. That woman could shonuff bake her ass off."

"You ain't never lied," agreed Chance, his mouth starting to water thinking about the sweets.

"Remember how she would dust them sugar cookies with just a sprinkle of cinnamon?"

"Nutmeg," corrected Chance.

"Whatever." X was a little perturbed by the correction of his memories.

"What you mean, whatever. I'm telling you the woman used nutmeg on her sugar cookies."

X had enough.

"What the hell do you know about baked goods? Hell, your mama always served them hard ass Buckeye sandwich cookies. The woman wouldn't even spring for Oreos. Naw, she had to serve some cheap ass bargain brand cookies right out the bag," said X.

"Alright, I concede the point. But you have to admit my Moms could get down on a pitcher of Kool Aid."

Chance and X exploded in laughter.

X, still unable to get comfortable, uncrossed his lanky legs and stretched them out in front of him. Leaning back on his elbows he watched the wisps of clouds swirl across the sky. The two let a long silence settle in.

"Remember how O.D. 'bout shitted in his pants that night we rode through Murray Hill. Man, I tell you I was some kinda scared. I swear I was never so glad to get out of a place as I was to get off that Hill in one piece," said Chance, astounded by the clarity of his memory which seemed to fall into place with no conscious help from him.

"Biggie all nervous behind the wheel. Drunk ass Roach cracking jokes and you looking like the gawd damn grim reaper. Man I thought for sure you would shoot that white boy and we would end up battling every honky up in that neighborhood," continued Chance, his narration barely keeping up with the images flashing through his head.

X broke in on those images: "You know my daddy is white."

The words clicked off the pictures in Chance's head like the high pitched buzz of the emergency broadcast system. Chance was half expecting X to say "this is just a test. Had this been a real emergency..."

Chance started to speak, but X hushed him by shaking his head "No."

"Do you know how badly I wanted to kill that white boy that night? Man, Chance I could feel my heart beating in my trigger finger, beating so hard that it throbbed like they was going to explode. I probably would have killed him to if you and Roach hadn't had grabbed me." X sat silent before beginning again.

"You know my father had those big ass saucer eyes, just like the boy, that's what made me snap. Saw them eyes when he came up to the car calling us niggers and I couldn't stop myself. I couldn't stop myself." His voice was soft and had came from far away.

"You knew about your real father back then?" asked Chance, staring at the lids that had closed over X's eyes.

"To this day my momma ain't never admitted it to me. Even when I confronted her about it 15 years ago. I told her I had seen his picture in the cedar chest and read the letters it was attached to with rubber bands. I told her about the newspaper clippings I found in one of her old Bibles about him enlisting in the Army, then one about him getting married, and third about him getting promoted on his job and being transferred to his firm's West Coast office.

"He was one reason I went to California, I wanted to confront him, talk to him, but I never did. Stood in front of his house a couple times, but that is as far as I ever got. Finally, one of my uncles told me the story about how momma used to help one of her great aunts on her job working for this rich Italian family. Momma used to help her during the holidays and in the summer, that's how they met. She was 16 and he had just graduated from high school, anyway one thing led to another, my mom got pregnant, he got sent to the Army and her great aunt lost her job. The letters I found in the cedar chest were the ones he wrote her from the Army. The last one was dated April 25, 1952. One month later I was born."

Again silence descended on the pair.

"You started to tell me that story a long time ago, right before we graduated from Kennedy, didn't you?" Chance asked heaving out a deep breath and for the first time since sitting down his legs began to ache.

"Yeah, well," said X, tilting forward as he started to get up. Chance tapped at his knee and X remained seated.

"All that time we all spent together, all those years of hanging 'round each other, and we never really knew each other. None of us really talked, you know, about serious stuff about how we were feeling and what we were going through. Yeah, we talked alot of smack, bout girls, sports, this and that, but nothing really, you know, heartfelt."

"You asking me why I didn't confide in you? Why I kept that secret all these years?"

"No, X, its goes deeper than that. I guess I'm trying to understand why we didn't open up to each other. I mean, ain't that what friends are supposed to do?"

"Nobody wanted to take the risk, that's the long and short of it. None of us wanted to risk being different, we didn't want to give someone some ammunition that could be used against us, to ridicule us. We all wore this macho mask, trying hard to live up to the definition we had of being men. Hell, we were all too unsure about ourselves to feel sure about our friends," said X.

"So what's changed? How are we any different now?"

"Maybe nothing's changed. Maybe we're still the same people but just in older bodies. Man, I don't know. I just know I had been wanting to tell you about that part of me for almost 30 years and for some reason it just felt right today. I mean I ain't no psychologist, all this reminiscing and everything...it was just time, that's all, just time." X's voice trailed off.

"You ever wonder about Mavis?" Instantly, Chance could tell by the bewildered look on X's face, that he had been clumsy and had almost regretted opening this box, almost.

Recovering a bit X asked "Who?", but then stopped himself from heading in that direction.

"I'm sorry, Chance, I started to... Hell, I don't know what I started to do. But yes, I thought about her a few times, especially during my conversion to Islam and all."

It was if Chance wasn't really listening to his friend as he continued. "I think about her alot. I even picked up the phone to call her parents once or twice when I was in college to get in touch with her. Never did though. Over the years I thought about searching her out just to see how she was doing. Maybe after this I should track her down and call her?"

"For what?"

The coldness infusing X words caught Chance off guard and he didn't understand the change in attitude.

"What do you mean for, what?" Chance said defensively.

"I mean exactly what I said, for what? Why you want to talk to her after all these years? To see how she's doing, if she's happy and successful and then to tell her you're sorry? Who are you sorry for, Mavis or for yourself?

The words stung and Chance lashed back.

"I'm not the one who's got a lot to be sorry for. You, O.D., Roach and Bigs, y'all the ones, who, who," Chance struggled to find the right words. "Gang-banged her."

"Damn, Chance, you can't even be honest with yourself after all these years. We raped her. That's what it was so just tell it like it was and is."

"It's not about no we, I didn't do nothing."

"You're damn right," said X cutting in to stop Chance cold. "You didn't do a damn thing and that's what's been eating at you all these years. Just because you didn't get in on the G-A-N-G -B-A-N-G," X purposely drew out the word, "don't mean you didn't rape her. Mavis was your friend, she was your friend, she wasn't nobody to us but just another broad, but she was your friend and you didn't do nothing to help her."

"Yeah, I'm ashamed of myself now, and I feel bad for what I did," continued X, softening his tone. "But, back then, down in that basement, I really didn't think I was doing something wrong. Or maybe I just didn't allow myself to think about what I was doing. But what is done is done and there ain't no way to change the past."

"But, I still feel so bad about it. I don't know why I didn't try to stop it. I knew she wanted me to help her but, I just left, and I still can't forgive myself for that," said Chance.

"So what are you looking for, forgiveness? You want to tell Mavis you're sorry, and that you want her to forgive you, right? How's that helping Mavis? How is you looking her up going to do anything good for her? Man, save your pitiful ass little sorry, because sorry ain't never helped no one. Chance, let's get real and be honest with yourself this is all about you. This is about you trying to make yourself feel better."

Chance, feeling a burning in his nose that caused his eyes to water, considered his friends words before he finally nodded.

"Listen, brother," X went on. "There are some burdens we just have to bear to the end of our days. All we can do is make peace with God and then do what we can not to add to those burdens. That's all any of us can do."

Chance reached over and grabbed X's hand. The two men sat silent for a long while. Eventually Chance gave X's hand one hard squeeze and rose to his feet. He knocked the wrinkles from his pants with his palms.

"Man, I have to get my story written," said Chance, grunting hoarsely trying to recover his voice.

"Why don't you walk with me over to the bureau and wait for me while I pound out this article. Shouldn't take more than hour or so, then we can go out to dinner and catch up on things."

"Sounds like a plan to me," said X, his robes falling in place as he stood giving no sign that he had been sitting on the ground for the better part of an hour.

They filtered slowly through the crowd, which divided its attention between Farrakhan talking about secret codes, pyramids, mad scientists, and pregnant numbers, and their own knots of private conversation.

"I tell you, sometimes that brother gets off on hearing his own voice," observed X, gesturing to one of the big television screens where the minister lectured.

Along the four block walk to the Beacon Herald's Washington bureau, Chance and X were stopped several times by black women, young and old, who shook their hands, and told them how proud they were of them and of all the black men at the Million Man March.

"Y'all showed the world something today," said a grandmotherly woman, who bear hugged first Chance and then X.

"All these black men in one place and no trouble. You boys just made me so proud today," then she broke out in tears.

"God bless you. God bless you," she said dabbing at her eyes with a white lace handkerchief, and then shooing the two men away with the same handkerchief.

Chance's and X's spirits were so high that they could have floated up to the fifth floor of the National Press Building where the bureau was located.

Several white faces turned to look at Chance and X as they pushed through the glass doors. Those same faces quickly turned back to the bank of television screens.

"Epstein, you about ready to file your March story?" asked a burly, red face man, a pair a bifocals anchored to the end of a bulbous nose.

Epstein, a reed-thin man, a fringe of red hair circling his sun baked dome, his fingers dancing along the keys of a computer, answered.

"Just about there," said the thin man, not looking up from his VDT screen. "What number are we going with for the crowd estimate, two-hundred thousand, or two-hundred and fifty thousand." He emphasized the numbers in a voice much louder than necessary.

"Let's be generous and go with 250," boomed the nose.

"Did you get anything about the trouble, I think it was something about a scuffle with one of the vendors and a couple of the marchers," the fat man added.

"We got someone checking with the police on that now," piped up another reporter from across the room.

"Well, whatever you get on that, particularly if there were any arrests or injuries make sure you give it to Epstein. We want to get that pretty high up in the story," the nose said as he plopped back down in his chair. Pushing his glasses back up to his eyes with a fat finger he looked up at Chance.

"You just back from the rally? You see any trouble while you were out there?"

Chance felt X squeeze his shoulder.

"Be cool. Don't let them fuck with you," X whispered through his teeth.

"I'm fine, brother, ain't nobody and nothing spoiling this day," said Chance as he walked to a desk at the far end of the newsroom.

"I hear that, my brother," said X, slapping him five. "I hear that."